OLIVE OIL
BAKING

OLIVE OIL
BAKING

Heart-Healthy Recipes That Increase Good Cholesterol and Reduce Saturated Fats

Lisa A. Sheldon

CUMBERLAND HOUSE
NASHVILLE, TN

OLIVE OIL BAKING
Published by Cumberland House Publishing, Inc.
431 Harding Industrial Drive
Nashville, TN 37211

Cover design: JulesRulesDesign
Text design: Lisa Taylor

Library of Congress Cataloging-in-Publication Data

Sheldon, Lisa A.
  Olive oil baking : heart-healthy recipes that increase good cholesterol and reduce saturated fats / Lisa A. Sheldon.
     p. cm.
  Includes index.
  ISBN-13: 978-1-58182-586-2 (hardcover)
  ISBN-10: 1-58182-586-2 (hardcover)
  1. Cookery (Olive oil) 2. Pastry. I. Title.

TX819.O42S52 2007
641.6′463—dc22

                                                                              2007012201

Printed in China
1 2 3 4 5 6 7 — 13 12 11 10 09 08 07

For my daughters, Zavi and Anya

Contents

Acknowledgments

Thanks to Ron Pitkin, Lisa Taylor, and all the members of the Cumberland House Publishing team who helped my vision come to life.

Heartfelt appreciation and thanks to Mary Flynn, PhD, RD, LDN, for writing an extraordinary foreword that showcases her enthusiasm for olive oil and better health.

With gratitude to Alayne Ronnenberg, ScD, Professor of nutrition at UMass Amherst, for being an inspiring and thoughtful teacher and advisor.

Many thanks to Tom and Ginny Sheldon for all they do to enrich my life and the lives of my daughters and husband.

And, most importantly, thanks to my husband and best friend, Andy, whose confidence in me never wavered. This book would not have been possible without his support and love.

Foreword

Olive oil is probably one of the most fascinating foods on Earth. Its long history includes mythology, biblical references, and military conquest. The wild olive tree is thought to have originated in Asia Minor (modern Turkey), where its fruit first attracted human attention around eight thousand years ago (6000 BC). The olive tree made its way to Greece, and the Greeks brought it to Italy around 1500 BC. The Italians were responsible for the subsequent spread of the olive tree throughout the cultures surrounding the Mediterranean Sea. As the Roman Empire expanded, the olive tree was taken to be cultivated in areas of conquest.

Ancient writings and artwork indicate that the olive tree was revered, both because of the ability of the hardy tree to survive difficult conditions and for the usefulness of its wood and fruits. The tree could live for hundreds of years, growing in the harshest of conditions and continually producing fruit.

Although there is no record of exactly when it was first discovered that oil could be squeezed from the olive fruit, olive oil has been part of the diet of Mediterranean cultures for at least 5,000 years. Besides its culinary and nutritive value, the oil squeezed from the fruit was used as a light source, as medicine, and as perfume. The use of the oil in religious ceremonies continues to this day.

Among vegetable oils, olive oil production is uniquely "low-tech," as it can be produced by simple, mechanical crushing of the fruit. Modern science has added very little to the process. The ancient Romans contributed an efficient method for extracting the oil. While the modern equipment used by large producers today is more sophisticated, contemporary olive oil production is basically the same as during the time of the Roman Empire.

My interest in extra virgin olive oil began about twenty years ago when I first read about the results of the large Seven Countries Study. The study began in the late 1950s in an attempt to understand why heart disease rates varied so greatly around the world and was increasing so dramatically in some areas. Diet was one of several potential factors measured. The lowest rates of heart disease were found in men from the Greek island of Crete. Despite having similar levels of blood cholesterol to those of American men, the men from Crete had heart disease rates 90 percent lower than the Americans—and they ate a diet that drew more than 40 percent of its calories from fat, primarily extra virgin olive oil.

As I was reading the results of the Seven Countries Study, the low-fat diet craze was taking hold in the United States. Health professionals began recommending a diet low in overall fat as a way to prevent chronic disease and to lose weight. I was intrigued by the contradictory results from places like Greece, where a higher fat diet was actually associated with better health.

I realized then that all fats are probably not equal, either in health or harm. I began to read more studies and found a wealth of information pertaining to the health benefits of olive oil. There are published studies showing that people who eat diets that use olive oil as the main fat have lower rates of heart disease and some cancers, including breast cancer. Many of the studies show that the more extra virgin olive oil consumed, the lower the rates of disease.

The prevailing message about olive oil in the media has been that its health benefits are based on it being the most monounsaturated of food oils, preventing it from oxidizing like common, highly polyunsaturated seed oils such as soybean, corn, and safflower. If the health benefits of olive oil were due solely to the lower oxidation, however, olive oil might be interchangeable with canola oil, the next most monounsaturated of food oils. I disagree, and studies have supported the preference for olive oil.

The health benefits of olive oil go beyond its fat profile. There are studies indicating extra virgin olive oil's other benefits: it contains very high amounts of antioxidants, especially the antioxidant form of vitamin E, alpha tocopherol; it lowers fasting triglycerides and raises beneficial HDL cholesterol compared to lower fat diets; it lowers blood pressure; it lowers fasting blood glucose and insulin; it decreases inflammation by increasing nitric oxide production; like fish oil, it makes blood less likely to clot.

For a long time, I have instructed patients to use extra virgin olive oil as their primary (if not only) source of dietary fat. I started research on a diet I call a "plant-based olive oil diet." The diet has very little meat and a moderate amount of fat, with extra virgin olive oil as the main source of fat. I have been comparing my diet to lower fat diets, both for weight loss and improvement in risk factors for chronic diseases. I realized early on that most people in this country did not know how to make use of olive oil in their cooking, so I began collecting recipes. I found a few desserts, but it was a challenge to adjust traditional baking recipes to use extra virgin olive oil.

I welcome this book of baking recipes using extra virgin olive oil and plan to recommend it to my patients and study participants. These recipes will help make a delicious dessert a healthy end to a meal, and increase our olive oil intake.

—Mary Flynn, PhD, RD, LDN

Author's Preface

This cookbook is the result of the combination of three main "ingredients": my decision to go back to school to study nutrition, my love of baking, and the high profile success of the Mediterranean diet.

Many good cookbooks have been written recently about the health benefits of eating a Mediterranean diet, rich in olive oil and fresh vegetables. Around the same time that the Mediterranean diet became widely accepted, I decided to go back to school to get a degree in clinical nutrition. Soon after that, the idea came to me to try baking with olive oil to see if my favorite recipes could be given a healthy update while preserving (or enhancing) familiar tastes and textures. My initial attempts at applying elements of the Mediterranean diet to my cookies, muffins, and quick breads worked out very well, and this cookbook started taking shape.

I have always enjoyed all aspects of baking. As I began studying nutrition, however, it was impossible to ignore the basic problem with the traditional baked goods I enjoyed making for family and friends (but often denied myself): not only are the products basically empty calories, but the heavily processed ingredients they rely on tend to have negative health consequences.

My experience over the past few years has been that baked goods traditionally made with shortening, margarine, and butter can almost always be made with olive oil instead, without sacrificing richness or flavor. I also identified other kinds of healthy and easy ingredient substitutions that could be made, transforming guilty "treats" into healthier foods.

I have a boundless passion for this approach to good health and great baking, and I want to share it with everyone who enjoys baking. My hope is that every home baker who picks up this book will find it easy to use and packed with appealing recipes. Whether you have just a few favorite recipes you stick with or you are a fearless experimenter, *Olive Oil Baking* is certain to introduce healthier recipes into your kitchen.

The first line of defense against the ailments of modern life—like heart disease, Type II diabetes, and arthritis/inflammatory diseases—is the person who decides which foods end up in the shopping cart, on the dinner menu, in the freezer, and in the lunch box. This cookbook speaks especially to the family "quartermaster," whose decisions can have a big influence on personal and public health. We all know someone who loves our cooking but also struggles with diet-related health issues. The recipes and suggestions you will find in *Olive Oil Baking* will satisfy the doctor/dietitian, the dietary conscience, and the taste buds alike.

OLIVE OIL
BAKING

Chapter 1
Olive Oil, Nutrition, and Your Health

The verdict is in: olive oil should have a place in any healthy diet. Its powerful combination of monounsaturated fats and (in extra virgin oils) polyphenols and antioxidants makes it an important dietary tool in the fight against a variety of common, chronic diseases. In the high amounts typically found in the daily diet of Greek, Italian, and other Mediterranean cultures, olive oil's health benefits include improved blood chemistry; reduced arthritis symptoms; reduced risks of heart disease, colon/breast cancer, and osteoporosis; and slowed cell aging.

For many years, the simplistic message coming from some experts and repeated by the media was that low-fat diets were healthiest. However, that is starting to change as large scientific studies have concluded that different sources and types of fats have very different health impacts.

What makes the typical modern diet healthy or unhealthy is not the amount of fat we consume, but rather the fact that the different types of fats are often not in healthy proportions. Certain types of fats are overused, and other essential types are almost absent. Numerous well-designed studies have found that simple low-fat or low-cholesterol diets do not have the expected protective effects against chronic disease because they ignore achieving a balance among the essential types of fats. The largest "experiment" pointing to this is that average fat intake in places like the United States has been declining for decades, while the incidence of diet-related disease has been on the rise.

On the other hand, studies of the so-called "Mediterranean diet" show that many health benefits are associated with a plant-based, high-fiber, less-processed way of eating that emphasizes high-quality fats often lacking in our diet—in particular extra virgin olive oil. Extensive research on the Mediterranean diet and olive oil suggests that good nutrition advice should not recommend a simplistic reduction in fat intake. The take-home message should instead be to start looking for places in our diet where good fats can be substituted/added.

Understanding Dietary Fats

Dietary fats are certainly complex. Although we hear about only four or five kinds—trans, saturated, monounsaturated, polyunsaturated, and maybe omega-3 these days—there are actually almost two dozen common types of fatty acids. Adding to the confusion is the fact that most foods contain numerous types of fat, just in different degrees.

Although the connections between dietary fat, health, and disease have been studied for many years, it was only recently that nutrition studies began giving careful enough attention to the very different effects of the many different sources of fat in our diet. Here are a few key things to keep in mind when choosing oils/fats for baking:

• Trans fatty acids are almost non-existent naturally in whole foods and have no known nutritional value. Even small amounts greatly increase the risks of heart and artery disease. Partially hydrogenated margarines, shortenings, and refined oils long used in fast food or processed food (e.g., donuts, frozen fried foods, etc.) are a major culprit. In 2006, the U.S. Food and Drug Administration began requiring that food manufacturers disclose the amount of trans fats on their products' nutrition facts label. This has helped raise consumer awareness and has encouraged producers to reduce or eliminate trans fats in processed foods.

• Saturated fats and polyunsaturated fats of various kinds are necessary to good health, but in baked goods they can be a case of too much of a good thing. Diets containing too much of the common types of saturated fat (for example, meat and dairy) can lower "good" HDL cholesterol levels and increase "bad" LDL cholesterol levels. Replacing some of the saturated fat—butter, eggs—in baking recipes with the common types of polyunsaturated fats has its own problems, however. The current epidemic of diseases of inflammation may be linked to overconsumption of polyunsaturated fats in the form of seed/vegetable oils, due in part to their tendency to oxidize and also to their highly refined/processed nature.

• Monounsaturated fats have not been labeled as "essential" fatty acids because the body can make them (unlike other essential fatty acids). However, studies show that high-quality monounsaturated fats like extra virgin olive oil offer protection against the effects of heart and artery disease. Of course, extra virgin olive oil turns out to have many other health benefits, as outlined in the rest of this chapter.

The simple recommendation for at-home baking is to replace some of the saturated (or polyunsaturated) fat in the baked goods you currently eat with monounsaturated fats. This does not mean removing all butter recipes from your kitchen. (Butter is not a bad word in my book, or in my house, where it enjoys a privileged position next to the olive oil. Look for the best-tasting, highest-quality butter, which can be higher in vitamins.) Your goal could simply be to start using more virgin olive oil than butter. In addition to making changes in your baking practices, you should try making at home some baked goods you currently buy at the store.

Most of us are not going to eliminate baked goods from our lunch boxes, dessert plates, and cookie jars. However, we can eliminate many of the typical, unhealthy versions of cookies, cakes, bars, and muffins (as well as the bland, low-fat variations). A dessert baked with olive oil, and enjoyed in moderation, can be rich and healthy!

Olive Oil: Reducing Heart Disease Risk

Simple changes in your kitchen can have a big effect on your family's heart health. Interest among nutritionists in the potential heart-health benefits of the so-called "Mediterranean diet" has been around since the 1950s, and has grown quickly since the 1980s and 1990s as more evidence pointed to low rates of heart disease among numerous traditional Mediterranean cultures and communities. The critical dietary components were believed to be wine, good quality olive oil, and moderate-to-low saturated fat intake. Olive oil, in particular, was seen as having a wide array of positive health effects, presumably because of its uniquely high level of monounsaturated fats.

Blood chemistry/serum cholesterol

Saturated and trans fats both have the negative effect of increasing LDL cholesterol levels, while trans fats also have the dangerous effect of lowering HDL cholesterol. These two types of fats need to be limited in the diet in order to control serum LDL levels.

Monounsaturated fats, on the other hand, have the net positive effect of lowering LDL levels and maintaining or raising HDL levels. This is the direction we want to go in order to reduce risk for heart disease.

It's the polyphenols!

Recent studies indicate that it is not just the monounsaturated fats in olive oil that are heart-healthy. Other compounds found in extra virgin olive oil, known as polyphenols, may also play an important protective and healing role. Polyphenols are powerful antioxidants found in olive oil and some fresh fruits, vegetables, and teas. These compounds have strong anti-inflammatory, antioxidant, and anticoagulant actions and are vital to cellular health because they prevent damage from free radicals.

Blood vessel function

A critical element of heart health is the delicate single layer of cells inside blood vessels known as the endothelium. This layer of cells helps regulate blood flow, blood clot formation, and the "stickiness" of immune cells and platelets to the wall of the blood vessel. If the cells of the endothelium become damaged due to aging, free radicals, or an immune response, hardened deposits called plaques can form—which is one of the hallmarks of heart disease.

Plaques fill with LDL cholesterol, leading to increased stress on the blood vessel. When the flow of blood becomes impeded or totally blocked in some cases, a heart attack can result. In addition, the plaques can cause bleeding or formation of a blood clot, leading to stroke in the brain.

Olive oil, and specifically polyphenols, help to combat this process. A large study found that the higher a virgin olive oil is in polyphenols, the greater its impact on increasing levels of HDL cholesterol and preventing the free radical damage/oxidation of LDL cholesterol, the primary event in atherosclerosis plaque formation.

A number of European studies have demonstrated that diets high in polyphenol-rich olive oil significantly improved the function of blood vessels and decreased cardiovascular risk. Under normal conditions, the endothelium function in the blood vessels is diminished for several hours after a meal. However, researchers found that subjects given a meal containing extra virgin olive oil experienced improved endothelial function and integrity. The researchers also noted increased production of nitric oxide, which aids in the relaxation of the endothelium, rendering it less susceptible to damage. In addition, lower levels of damaging free radicals were present in study subjects' blood than is normally seen after a meal.

This research underscores the importance of not just increasing the amount of olive oil in our diet but, when possible, using good-quality olive oil, rich in polyphenols. Extra virgin olive oil—cold-pressed (hand-picked is best), stored at proper temperature away from sunlight and used while fresh—contains far more polyphenols than lower-grade or improperly stored products.

Lowering Blood Pressure

A diet known as Dietary Approaches to Stop Hypertension (DASH) is often recommended as an important step in managing blood pressure. This diet is rich in important nutrients and fiber and contains far more electrolytes, potassium, calcium, and magnesium than are found in the average diet. It also suggests reducing saturated fat; including some calcium-rich, low-fat dairy products; and when choosing oils/fats for cooking, selecting a highly monounsaturated oil, such as olive oil.

One study has reported a reduced need for anti-hypertension medication in people with a high intake of extra virgin olive oil. Greek investigators found that, while the Mediterranean diet as a whole reduces blood pressure in a healthy population, olive oil is primarily responsible for the Mediterranean diet's beneficial effects. Higher consumption of olive oil, vegetables, or fruit was associated with lower blood pressure. On the other hand, higher consumption of carbohydrates, meat, or alcohol was associated with higher blood pressure.

Lowering Cancer Risk

Breast cancer: The key to olive oil's impact on breast cancer reduction lies in oleic acid, which is the main component of olive oil. Research has shown that oleic acid blocks the action of a cancer-causing gene found in about 30 percent of breast cancer patients. Also, oleic acid increased the effectiveness of drug treatments aimed at suppression of this particular gene.

Studies in Spanish, Greek, and Italian populations found a 25 percent reduction in the risk of breast cancer for women who consumed a diet high in olive oil compared with women who consumed a diet rich in other types of oils and fats.

Colon cancer: Based on studies examining colon cancer, researchers believe that the combination of oleic acid and polyphenols are the key to prevention. Research suggests that a mixture of polyphenols could protect against colon cancer. Laboratory studies have found that olive oil phenols led to significant reduction in the invasiveness of a colon cancer cell line. The anti-inflammatory, antioxidant, and anticoagulant aspects of olive oil's polyphenols may play a role.

In a laboratory study, animals fed a diet supplemented with olive oil had a lower risk of colon cancer than those fed safflower oil–supplemented diets. Olive oil's protective benefits against colon cancer appeared almost as great as the benefits of fish oils, which several studies have linked to a reduction in colon cancer risk.

Reducing Arthritis and Inflammatory Disease

A recent article outlines the important anti-inflammatory/anti-arthritis properties associated with olive oil. Researchers have found that oleocanthal, a compound in olive oil, prevents the production of pro-inflammatory COX-1 and COX-2 enzymes—the same way that NSAID drugs like ibuprofen work. Rather than always reaching for the medicine bottle, reach for the extra virgin olive oil!

The investigators found that individuals who consumed the least amount of olive oil over their lifetime were 2.5 times more likely to develop rheumatoid arthritis than those who consumed the most olive oil. In addition, subjects who consumed the most cooked vegetables had a 75 percent lower risk of developing rheumatoid arthritis.

The typical American diet is high in the types of fat that are broken down into hormones which promote inflammation. The fatty acids in olive oil, on the other hand, are broken down to hormones that inhibit inflammation.

Olive Oil and Your Skin: Slowing the Aging Process

Scientists have long held that the reason we show the effects of aging is oxidative damage to our cells. So throw away your petroleum-based skin care products! A better way to combat the effects of the aging process is a diet rich in antioxidants, such as vitamins and minerals. Olive oil, rich in antioxidant properties, is a natural choice.

For centuries, olive oil has been used not only in healthy diets but also to add moisture and glow to skin, hair, and nails. A small amount of olive oil massaged into dry hands, elbows, and heels is a completely natural moisturizer, containing no added chemicals or fragrances. It is also a great natural remedy for dry, chapped lips. And a few tablespoons in the shower, or added to your bath water, will moisturize and nourish your skin.

To perk up dry, damaged, or processed hair, massage 2–3 tablespoons of olive oil into your scalp and the roots of your hair during your shower, allowing it to penetrate for several minutes. Then wash as usual. You are certain to notice the difference!

Managing Blood Glucose/Insulin Recognition

If you are at risk for diabetes, it is important to look at the types of fat in your diet. Studies in diabetic patients have shown that diets containing olive oil had better effects on blood sugar than meals that were simply low in fat. In addition, adding olive oil to a good diabetic diet helps to keep triglyceride levels low. Triglyceride levels tend to be high in diabetic patients, contributing to heart disease risk.

Reducing Osteoporosis Risks

Osteoporosis, or porous bone disease, is characterized by deterioration and weakening of bone tissue. This leads to increased incidence of fractures, especially of the hip, spine, and wrist.

Very promising new research is showing that the polyphenols in olives have shown remarkable bone-sparing properties. People eating a traditional Mediterranean diet have a much lower incidence of osteoporosis than those consuming a typical Western diet.

Two polyphenols in particular, oleuropin and hydroxytyrosol, greatly reduce inflammation-mediated bone loss, one of the main contributors to osteoporosis in older people, especially in women with estrogen hormone deficiency. In the experiment, osteoporotic animals fed with oleuropin recovered about 70–75 percent of their bone density, a 50 percent improvement over those that were not fed the supplement.

Conclusions

In recent years the culinary and medical establishments have embraced the use of olive oil for its warm, aromatic taste and its extraordinary health benefits.

Eaten raw—for example, on salads—or used in cooking, extra virgin olive oil is one of the healthiest foods. Rich in monounsaturated fatty acids as well as polyphenols, it has powerful anti-inflammatory, antioxidant, and anticoagulant properties. Hard evidence is beginning to show that olive oil helps reduce rates of heart disease, atherosclerosis, diabetes, and colon cancer and improves blood chemistry.

After reading the ways in which olive oil can be beneficial to your health and trying some of the great baking recipes in this cookbook, you may be inclined to go a step further in making over other parts of your diet. There are nearly unlimited health benefits to adopting a Mediterranean-style diet. And preparing and enjoying these healthy meals together as a family will help children and teenagers learn basic principles of healthy nutrition.

Chapter 2
Selection and Storage of Olive Oils

Choosing a good extra virgin oil should not be an anxiety-producing experience. Experimentation is the key. The flavor and character of olive oils is diverse, and there are sure to be ones that will stand out to you. So taste a few kinds plain, on vegetables, with a piece of bread, and in your baking recipes, and then choose the one(s) you like best!

The Basics

• The flavorful spices, fruits, chocolate, and extracts in baked goods are not affected by the smooth flavor of extra virgin olive oil. There is no need to purchase a flavorless "mild" or "light" olive oil for baking.

• Like most cooks, I look for bargains when shopping but avoid some cheap ingredients (e.g., meat, butter, vanilla, and eggs). Research shows that plain old olive oil has health benefits, but high-quality extra virgin olive oil has greatly increased benefits.

• Bakers rarely taste key ingredients raw—vanilla extract, flour, cinnamon, etc. Tasting extra virgin olive oils is definitely recommended (and good for you). To truly appreciate variations in flavor, try a little plain first (before using a bread or green of questionable flavor). In Europe, olive oil taste has long been evaluated just like wine. Expect a smooth texture, a fruity flavor, and a delayed tingling in your throat.

• Good indicators of quality are if the oil is organic and/or unfiltered, has very low acidity (less than 1 percent), or if the olives are from a particular, named orchard or region (e.g., Crete, Tuscany, Sonoma). Usually these oils will be found in half-liter bottles (not gallon containers).

• As of 2007, the U.S. market does not restrict the use of the term "extra virgin,"—so by itself, the term is not a good guarantee of quality. Look for certified extra virgin olive oil almost exclusively (COOC for California; DOP for Italy; black rooster label for the Chianti region of Tuscany; DO for Spain; HEPO for Greece; and various organic certifiers).

• Good extra virgin olive oil requires more than good olives. To maximize the freshness, flavors, and benefits of the oil, producers follow rigorous procedures: careful (often hand-) harvesting and prompt processing (including transportation, fruit storage, crushing/pressing, solids separation, and oil storage in an oxygen-free container). Expect to spend more for carefully tended olive oil.

Labeling

You will find different grades and descriptions of olive oil in large markets, so let's take a look at what's behind the labels:

- Virgin oils are produced by a single, simple pressing:
  - Extra virgin—Since there are currently no controls applied to labeling of olive oil sold in the U.S., tasting olive oils is important. Extra virgin oil tastes smooth and slightly fruity, and the healthy phenols will tingle the back of your throat. Color can vary, from champagne to green-golden to bright green.
  - Fine virgin olive oil is slightly lower quality, but these oils can still have a full, smooth flavor and all of the health benefits.
- Refined and blended oils—Most mainstream oils found in supermarkets in the U.S. are inexpensive imports blended from many oils. Blends based on refined oils will not have the additional health benefits because components like polyphenols found naturally in the oil have been refined out.
  - "Pure" olive oil—Don't be fooled by the label, as "pure" actually means the oil is a blend of refined oil and a small amount of virgin oil to add some flavor. Some low-quality oils have been found to be mixed with other types of oils, e.g., common vegetable oils.
  - Filtered versus unfiltered—Unfiltered extra virgin olive oil actually lasts much longer and may have more health benefits. Filtering does not initially affect the taste of the oil. Unfiltered extra virgin oil is not as clear, as it contains tiny suspended particles of the olive. Note that the terms "filtered" and "unfiltered" are applied to *non-virgin* oil too.

Containers and Storage

Good olive oil has very good storage characteristics compared to polyunsaturated oils of similar quality. Olive oil's monounsaturated fats are very stable and heat-resistant, but it should still be stored properly and used within 6 to 12 months to ensure its healthy phytonutrients remain intact and available. Proper storage of good olive oil is like garaging a fine car—you are protecting your investment.

At the market, try to find olive oil sold in dark tinted bottles or small tins. Proper packaging is the first line of defense against the damage caused by exposure to light, heat, and oxygen. Purchase oil in tinted glass containers at the back of the shelf, out of direct light and away from heat sources. Choosing tinted glass, ceramic, or metal containers preserves extra virgin olive oil's beneficial compounds. Italian researchers compared oils stored in the light to those stored in the dark for twelve months. Oils stored in clear bottles under supermarket lighting lost at least 30 percent of their Vitamin E and carotenoids. Within just two months, olive oil exposed to light and air will form enough free radicals that it can no longer be classified as extra virgin.

If you find you use olive oil slowly, buy it in smaller containers. Usually, good-quality olive oil is found in half-liter (500 mL) bottles. If you enjoy having the olive oil on the counter for ease of use, transfer it to a colored or opaque container that will limit light exposure, which can degrade and lessen the healthful properties of the oil.

When you get home, store the olive oil in a dark cabinet. You do not need to store oil in the refrigerator. If you do, it will congeal and acquire a gel-like consistency. Just leave it at room temperature for half an hour, and it will return to its liquid state, however.

Also check the date on the container before buying. Unlike fine wines, olive oil's taste does not improve with age. The fresher the better.

CHAPTER 3
CAKES & DESSERTS

Almond Coconut Bundt Cake

A one-ounce serving of almonds contains the same amount of flavonoids—powerful antioxidants—as a serving of broccoli or a cup of brewed black or green tea. Almonds are also an excellent source of vitamin E and calcium.

I cup whole almonds, toasted and chopped	I cup reduced-fat or fat-free sour cream
I¼ cups sweetened flaked coconut, toasted	⅓ cup olive oil
I cup all-purpose flour	¾ cup granulated sugar
½ cup whole wheat pastry flour	2 eggs
½ teaspoon baking soda	I teaspoon almond extract
½ teaspoon baking powder	I teaspoon vanilla extract
¾ teaspoon salt	¾ cup mini chocolate chips

To toast the almonds: Heat oven to 300°F. Place almonds on a small baking sheet and bake 10–15 minutes, stirring once, until aromatic and skins begin to crack slightly. Set aside to cool, and then chop finely.

To toast the coconut: Place shredded coconut on baking sheet and bake for 8–12 minutes at 300°F, stirring twice. Remove from oven when toasted and slightly brown. Cool.

Increase oven temperature to 350°F. Coat a 12-cup Bundt pan with cooking spray or oil.

In a large bowl, combine flours, baking soda, baking powder, and salt.

In a medium bowl, whisk together sour cream, olive oil, sugar, eggs, and almond and vanilla extracts. Whisk until smooth. Add wet ingredients to the dry and stir just until blended. Stir in chopped almonds, coconut, and chocolate chips. Spread into prepared Bundt pan.

Bake for 30–35 minutes or until a toothpick inserted into the center of the cake comes out clean.

Cool the cake in the pan on a wire rack for 15 minutes before inverting cake onto rack. Cool completely.

Serves 14–16.

Apple Crisp

Granny Smith, Gravenstein, Cortland, or Macintosh are all great choices for this classic fall dish!

8	cups peeled, cored, and thinly sliced apples	¾	cup all-purpose flour
½	cup granulated sugar	¾	cup brown sugar
2	teaspoons cinnamon	½	cup olive oil
1¼	cups old-fashioned rolled oats (not quick- cooking)	1½	teaspoons vanilla extract
		¾	cup chopped walnuts (optional)

Preheat oven to 350°F.

To prepare the filling: Place apple slices in a large bowl, sprinkle with granulated sugar and cinnamon and toss to evenly coat the apples. Set aside.

To prepare the topping: In a medium bowl, combine the oats, flour, and brown sugar. After these ingredients have been mixed together, make a well in the center and add olive oil and vanilla extract. Rub the mixture together with fingers until it starts to come together and form a crumb-like texture. Add walnuts to the topping mixture if desired.

Transfer apple slices to a 9 x 13-inch baking dish. Sprinkle topping evenly over the apples.

Bake at 350°F for 1 hour or until the apples are tender when pierced with a paring knife.

Cool pan 10–15 minutes on a wire rack. Serve warm, with ice cream or whipped cream if desired.

Makes 10 servings.

DAIRY-FREE/VEGAN

Banana Date Cake
with Cream Cheese Frosting

This cake is scrumptious with or without the frosting. For a different presentation, create a fancy design with a cake stencil and confectioners' sugar. To make your own cake stencil, use an Exacto® knife to cut a stiff piece of paper into a snowflake or other design. Lay stencil on top of the cake and dust with powdered sugar from a sieve. Use care in lifting the stencil from the cake so the pattern is not disturbed. Apply the stencil right before service.

I	cup whole wheat pastry flour	⅓	cup low-fat buttermilk
I½	cups all-purpose flour	I	teaspoon vanilla extract
I	teaspoon baking powder	¼	teaspoon almond extract
¼	teaspoon baking soda	I	(10-ounce) package chopped dates
½	teaspoon salt	¾	cup chopped walnuts
⅓	cup olive oil		*Frosting:*
I	whole egg	I	(8-ounce) package low-fat or fat-free
I	egg white		cream cheese, at room temperature
½	cup granulated sugar	½	cup powdered sugar, sifted
½	cup light brown sugar, packed	½	teaspoon vanilla extract
I½	cups ripe mashed banana		

Preheat oven to 375°F. Coat 9 x 13-inch glass baking dish with cooking spray.

In a medium bowl, combine flours, baking powder, baking soda, and salt.

In a large bowl, combine olive oil, whole egg, egg white, and both sugars. Add the mashed banana, buttermilk, and almond and vanilla extracts and mix well. Add the dry ingredients to the wet and stir until just moistened. Add the chopped dates and walnuts and gently combine.

Pour the batter into prepared dish. Bake for 20–25 minutes or until the top springs back when touched.

Cool the cake in the dish on a wire rack.

To prepare the frosting: Place the cream cheese, powdered sugar, and vanilla extract in a small mixing bowl and beat with a handheld mixer until light and fluffy.

Refrigerate leftovers.

Makes 12–16 servings.

Caramel Apple Upside-Down Cake

While this cake looks impressive, it is easy to make and can be whipped up in a hurry for unexpected guests. Imagine their arrival in a home warmed by the scent of apples and cinnamon—they will feel truly special!

⅓	cup caramel topping	½	teaspoon salt
2	cups peeled, thinly sliced apples (Granny Smith or other tart variety)	½	cup low-fat buttermilk, shaken
¾	cup all-purpose flour	1	teaspoon vanilla extract
½	cup whole wheat pastry flour	⅔	cup brown sugar, packed
¼	cup wheat germ	5	tablespoons olive oil
½	teaspoon baking soda	2	eggs
1	teaspoon cinnamon	½	cup unsweetened applesauce

Preheat the oven to 350°F and coat a 9-inch square baking dish with cooking spray.

Drizzle the bottom of the pan with the caramel topping—it will not coat the bottom completely. Layer in the apple slices, overlapping evenly.

In a large bowl, combine the flours, wheat germ, baking soda, cinnamon, and salt.

In another large bowl, whisk together the buttermilk, vanilla extract, brown sugar, olive oil, and eggs until smooth. Add the applesauce and whisk until well blended.

Add the wet ingredients to the dry and stir just until combined. Pour the batter over the apple slices.

Bake for 35 minutes or until a toothpick inserted into the center of the cake comes out clean.

Cool in the pan on a wire rack for 10 minutes. To remove from the pan, place a plate upside down on the top of the cake and invert. Serve warm.

Serves 9–12.

Carrot Cake

This cake is perfect by itself. But if you would prefer some accompaniment, make the tangy whipped cream recipe that follows and serve on the side.

1½ cups almonds, toasted and ground to almond meal
1 cup whole wheat pastry flour
1¼ cups all-purpose flour
1 tablespoon baking powder
1½ teaspoons cinnamon
½ teaspoon allspice
½ teaspoon salt
4 large eggs
1 cup pure maple syrup
¼ cup olive oil
½ cup unsweetened applesauce

½ cup low-fat or fat-free sour cream
1 teaspoon vanilla extract
1 teaspoon almond extract
½ teaspoon maple extract
2 cups finely grated carrots
1 cup raisins or currants or a combination of both

Tangy Whipped Cream:
½ cup heavy cream
¼ teaspoon vanilla extract
1 cup low-fat or fat-free lemon yogurt

To toast the almonds: Place almonds on a baking sheet and bake at 300°F for 10–15 minutes or until aromatic and the skins begin to crack slightly. Set aside to cool. After they are cool, grind almonds in a food processor or blender until a fine meal texture is achieved, similar to corn meal.

Preheat the oven to 350°F and coat a 9 x 13-inch glass baking dish with cooking spray.

In a large bowl, combine the flours, ground almonds, baking powder, cinnamon, allspice, and salt. Make a well in the center.

In a medium bowl, whisk together the eggs, maple syrup, olive oil, applesauce, and sour cream. Add the three extracts and mix again. Stir in carrots.

Pour the wet ingredients into the well in the center of the dry ingredients and stir just until almost combined. Then add the raisins or currants and continue stirring just until moistened. Transfer the batter to the prepared pan.

Bake at 350°F for 35–40 minutes or until a toothpick inserted into the center of the cake comes out clean. Cool on a wire rack.

Tangy Whipped Cream: Whip heavy cream and vanilla extract until stiff peaks form. Then gently fold in the lemon yogurt.

Serves 16–20.

Chocolate Coconut Almond Cupcakes

Don't save this recipe just for birthdays and special events. These delicious little cakes are perfect for an elegant dinner party or a picnic. Because they are so easy to make, you can always whip them up in a pinch.

½ cup toasted almonds, finely chopped and cooled

1 cup toasted coconut, cooled

1 cup plus 1 tablespoon all-purpose flour

½ teaspoon baking soda

¼ teaspoon salt

½ cup olive oil

3 ounces unsweetened chocolate, chopped

½ cup strong brewed coffee, room temperature

2 tablespoons coconut rum or white rum

1 teaspoon vanilla extract

1 egg, beaten

1 cup granulated sugar

Powdered sugar for dusting (optional)

To toast the almonds: Heat oven to 300°F. Place almonds on a small baking sheet and bake 10–15 minutes, stirring once, until aromatic and skins begin to crack slightly. Set aside to cool, and then chop finely.

To toast the coconut: Place shredded coconut on baking sheet and bake for 8–12 minutes at 300°F, stirring twice. Remove from oven when toasted and slightly brown. Cool.

Increase oven temperature to 350°F. Line a 12-cup muffin tin with paper liners.

In a small bowl, mix together flour, baking soda, and salt. Set aside.

In a heavy, medium-sized saucepan, heat olive oil and chopped chocolate over low heat. Once chocolate is melted and mixture is smooth, remove from the heat. Add the coffee, rum, and vanilla extract; whisk until well blended. Add egg and sugar. Add flour mixture and whisk until smooth.

Using a large spoon stir in toasted almonds and coconut. Divide the batter among the prepared muffin cups.

Bake for 25–30 minutes or until a toothpick inserted into the middle of a cupcake comes out clean.

Allow to cool in pan for 2 minutes, then transfer to a wire rack. Dust with powered sugar if desired.

Store in an airtight container at room temperature for up to 3 days.

Makes 12 cupcakes.

DAIRY-FREE

Chocolate Coconut Almond Cupcakes

Coconut Layer Cake

This is the quintessential coconut cake and, boy, is it ever a showstopper. Great for a birthday or party, this is one cake your guests won't forget!

I	tablespoon all-purpose flour		I	recipe Fluffy Coconut Frosting (see below)
2¼	cups all-purpose flour		⅔	cup flaked sweetened coconut, divided
2¼	teaspoons baking powder			
½	teaspoon salt			*Fluffy Coconut Frosting:*
I⅔	cups sugar		4	large egg whites
¼	cup olive oil		½	teaspoon cream of tartar
3	large eggs			Dash of salt
I	(14-ounce) can light coconut milk, shaken/stirred		I	cup granulated sugar
			¼	cup water
2	teaspoons vanilla extract		½	teaspoon vanilla extract
I	teaspoon coconut extract		¼	teaspoon coconut extract

Preheat oven to 350°F. Coat two 9-inch round cake pans with cooking spray or oil. Dust with I tablespoon flour, knocking out excess.

In a medium bowl, combine 2¼ cups flour, baking powder, and salt, stirring with a whisk.

Place sugar and olive oil in a large bowl and beat with a handheld mixer at medium speed until well blended. Add eggs, one at a time, beating well after each addition. Beat in vanilla and coconut extracts. Add some of flour mixture and coconut milk alternately to sugar mixture, beginning and ending with flour mixture, beating between additions.

Pour batter into prepared pans. Bake for 30 minutes or until a toothpick inserted in the center comes out clean. Cool in pans 10 minutes on wire racks, and then remove from pans onto rack. Cool completely.

To make the frosting: Place egg whites, cream of tartar, and salt in a large bowl; beat with a mixer at high speed until stiff peaks form. Bring sugar and water to a boil in a saucepan. Cook, without stirring, until candy thermometer registers 238°F. Pour hot sugar syrup in a thin stream over egg whites, beating at high speed. Stir in extracts. Cool slightly.

Place one cake layer on a plate; spread with I cup of cooled Fluffy Coconut Frosting. Sprinkle with ⅓ cup coconut. Top with remaining cake layer; spread remaining frosting over top and sides of cake. Sprinkle remaining ⅓ cup coconut over top of cake. Store cake, loosely covered, in refrigerator.

Serves 12–16.

DAIRY FREE

Cranberry Apple Butter Spice Cake

The sweetness of the apple butter balances with the tartness from the cranberries in this beautiful Bundt cake.

1¼	cups all-purpose flour		1	egg
1	cup whole wheat pastry flour		¾	cup brown sugar, packed
2	teaspoons cinnamon		⅓	cup olive oil
2	teaspoons ground ginger		½	cup low-fat milk
½	teaspoon allspice		1	cup apple butter
¼	teaspoon nutmeg		2	teaspoons vanilla extract
1½	teaspoons baking powder		1	cup fresh cranberries, chopped fine
1	teaspoon baking soda		½	cup chopped walnuts
1	teaspoon salt			

Preheat the oven to 350°F and coat a 12-cup Bundt pan with cooking spray or oil.

In a medium bowl combine the flours, cinnamon, ginger, allspice, nutmeg, baking powder, baking soda, and salt.

In a large bowl, beat the egg and brown sugar with a handheld mixer until light and fluffy. Add the olive oil and beat for 2 minutes. Stir in the milk, apple butter, and vanilla extract.

Add the dry ingredients to the wet and with a few broad strokes start to combine, then add the cranberries and walnuts. Continue stirring until just combined.

Transfer the batter to the prepared pan.

Bake for 60–65 minutes or until a toothpick inserted into the center of the cake comes out clean.

Cool in the pan on a wire rack for 15 minutes before inverting cake onto rack for removal. Cool completely.

Serves 12–16.

Cranberry Walnut Pound Cake

Cranberries add a touch of tartness to this wonderfully rich and aromatic cake. The specks of red add a festive touch at the holidays or any time of the year. Cranberries freeze well, so pick up an extra bag in season (fall) and throw them in the freezer for the rest of the year.

I	cup all-purpose flour		I⅓	cups granulated sugar
I	cup whole wheat pastry flour		½	cup olive oil
½	teaspoon baking powder		I	teaspoon vanilla extract
¼	teaspoon baking soda		½	cup non-fat or low-fat sour cream
I	teaspoon salt		½	cup finely chopped walnuts
¼	teaspoon cinnamon		¾	cup fresh cranberries, finely chopped
4	large eggs			

Preheat the oven to 350°F. Generously coat a Bundt pan with cooking spray or oil.

In a small bowl, combine the flours, baking powder, baking soda, salt, and cinnamon.

In a large bowl, beat the eggs with a handheld mixer until light and slightly increased in volume. Add the sugar slowly while continuing to beat. The mixture will become light and fluffy. Add the olive oil and vanilla extract and beat another 2 minutes.

Alternately add the dry ingredients and the sour cream to the batter, beating between additions. Gently fold in the chopped nuts and cranberries.

Transfer the batter to the prepared pan.

Bake at 350°F for 60–65 minutes or until a toothpick inserted into the center comes out clean.

Cool in the pan on a wire rack for 10 minutes. Then invert the pan onto rack to remove and cool completely.

Serves 12–16.

Fruit and Cream Pizza

This dessert is sure to impress. You can use well-drained canned or fresh fruit depending on what is in season. Create your own masterpiece!

Crust:

1	cup whole wheat pastry flour
3	tablespoons granulated sugar
3	tablespoons very finely chopped or ground almonds
1/8	teaspoon ground nutmeg
1	teaspoon grated orange peel
1/4	cup low-fat buttermilk, shaken
2	tablespoons olive oil

Filling:

6	ounces low-fat cream cheese, room temperature
1/3	cup powdered sugar
1	teaspoon cornstarch
1	tablespoon fresh lemon juice
1	teaspoon vanilla extract

Fruits: *

1	cup sliced fresh strawberries
2	kiwi fruits, peeled and sliced
2	nectarines, sliced

Preheat the oven to 400°F.

To make the crust: Combine the flour, sugar, almonds, and nutmeg in a bowl. In another bowl whisk together the orange peel, buttermilk, and olive oil. Pour the wet ingredients into the dry and stir just until the dough starts to form. If dough seems too dry add a few drops of buttermilk at a time until it is the right consistency.

Transfer the dough to a work surface or pastry board sprinkled lightly with flour (or place on a piece of parchment paper). Form a ball with a few quick kneading motions. Roll the dough out to a thickness of 1/4 inch and about 9–10 inches in diameter. Transfer the dough to a baking sheet lined with parchment paper. Fold the edge over toward the center of the circle, overlapping only 1/2 an inch of dough to form the edge crust. Poke the crust with a fork all over.

Bake the crust for 10–12 minutes or until it is lightly browned. Allow the crust to cool on the baking sheet.

To make the filling: Combine all of the filling ingredients in a small bowl and beat for 2–4 minutes using a handheld mixer until well-combined and light. Spread the filling on the prepared crust and refrigerate for at least 1 hour, or up to 4 hours, covered. After it has chilled, top with the fruit in a decorative pattern and refrigerate at least 1 hour.

*Note: Other fruit blends that work well: 1 cup fresh pineapple, cut into chunks; 1 small can of mandarin oranges, well-drained; 1/2 cup fresh blueberries.

Serves 10–12.

Hearty Gingerbread

Gingerbread is a treat year-round, so don't wait for cool weather to make this old-fashioned family favorite!

I	cup all-purpose flour	½	teaspoon salt
I	cup whole wheat pastry flour	¾	cup low-fat buttermilk, shaken
I½	teaspoons ground ginger	½	cup granulated sugar
2	teaspoons ground cinnamon	½	cup molasses
½	teaspoon cloves	¼	cup low-fat milk
I	teaspoon baking powder	¼	cup olive oil
I	teaspoon baking soda	2	large eggs
¼	cup finely minced crystallized ginger		

Preheat oven to 350°. Coat either a 9-inch square or a 7 x 11-inch glass baking dish with cooking spray.

In a large bowl, combine the flours, ground ginger, cinnamon, cloves, baking powder, baking soda, and crystallized ginger and salt, stirring well with a whisk; make a well in center of mixture.

In a large bowl, combine buttermilk, sugar, molasses, milk, olive oil, and eggs and stir well with a whisk. Add buttermilk mixture to flour mixture, stirring just until moist.

Transfer batter into prepared baking dish.

Bake for 45 minutes or until a toothpick inserted in center of cake comes out clean. Cool in dish for 10 minutes on a wire rack; remove from pan. Cool completely on wire rack.

Store in a covered container for up to 5 days or freeze for 1 month.

Makes 10–12 servings.

Lemon Chiffon Cake with Blueberry Sauce

This light and dreamy cake is low in fat, elegant and easy to make. A great summer dessert!

1	cup sifted cake flour		½	teaspoon lemon extract
½	cup granulated sugar		2	large egg yolks
1	teaspoon baking powder		6	large egg whites (at room temperature)
¼	teaspoon salt		¼	teaspoon cream of tartar
2	tablespoons olive oil		*Blueberry sauce:*	
1	tablespoon grated lemon rind		2	cups fresh or frozen blueberries
¼	cup fresh lemon juice		2	teaspoons corn starch
1	teaspoon vanilla extract		½	cup granulated sugar

Preheat oven to 350°F.

In a large bowl, combine flour, sugar, baking powder, and salt; stir well. Add olive oil, lemon rind, lemon juice, vanilla and lemon extracts, and egg yolks; beat mixture at medium speed with a handheld mixer until smooth.

Using clean, dry beaters, beat egg whites and cream of tartar at high speed with a handheld mixer until stiff peaks form. Gently fold one-fourth of egg white mixture into batter until lightened and no areas of egg whites are visible. Carefully fold in remaining egg white mixture.

Pour batter into an ungreased 10-inch tube or Bundt pan, spreading evenly. Run a paring knife through the batter to break any air pockets in the cake.

Bake for 25 minutes or until cake springs back when lightly touched. Let cool for 40 minutes, inverting pan. Loosen cake from sides of pan using a narrow metal spatula. Invert cake onto a cake plate.

Serve cake with blueberry sauce (below) on the side.

To make the blueberry sauce: Combine blueberries, corn starch, and sugar in a heavy saucepan. Slowly bring to a bare simmer, stirring often. When the berries begin to thicken and take on a slightly darkened appearance remove from the heat and allow to cool in the pan. Can be made up to 2 days ahead.

Serves 8–10.

DAIRY-FREE

Lemon Chiffon Cake

Lemon Poppy Seed Pound Cake

This cake has just a fraction of the fat found in a traditional pound cake, but you won't know the difference. It is moist and slightly dense, just what you would expect from a pound cake. It is wonderful served with fresh blueberries or peaches.

1	cup all-purpose flour	1	tablespoon lemon zest
1	cup whole wheat pastry flour	3	tablespoons fresh lemon juice
½	teaspoon baking powder	1	teaspoon vanilla extract
¼	teaspoon baking soda	½	cup non-fat or low-fat sour cream
1	teaspoon salt		*Glaze (optional):*
2	tablespoons poppy seeds	2	tablespoons lemon juice
4	large eggs	1-1½	cups powdered sugar
1⅓	cups granulated sugar	¼	teaspoon vanilla extract
½	cup olive oil		

Preheat the oven to 350°F. Generously spray a Bundt pan with cooking spray.

In a small bowl, combine the flours, baking powder, baking soda, salt, and poppy seeds.

In a large bowl, beat the eggs with a handheld mixer until light and slightly increased in volume. Add the sugar slowly while continuing to beat. The mixture will become light and fluffy. Add the olive oil, lemon zest, lemon juice, and vanilla extract and beat another 2 minutes.

Alternately add the dry ingredients and the sour cream to the batter, beating between additions.

Transfer the batter to the prepared pan and bake for 55–60 minutes or until a toothpick inserted into the center comes out clean.

Cool in the pan on a wire rack for 10 minutes. Then invert the pan to remove and cool completely on a wire rack.

Simple glaze for the cake (optional): Whisk the lemon juice, powdered sugar, and vanilla extract in a small bowl until the mixture has a smooth consistency. Drizzle over the cake.

Serves 12–16.

Maple Spice Cake

Maple flavor is warm and sensual yet subtle. This cake's delicate maple flavor is enhanced with spice and molasses to bring out added dimension and complexity. Serve with warm cider or some apple slices; it's great with peaches, too.

1 cup all-purpose flour	¼ cup olive oil
½ cup whole wheat pastry flour	1 tablespoon molasses
1 teaspoon baking soda	1 teaspoon vanilla extract
1¼ teaspoons baking powder	½ teaspoon maple extract
½ teaspoon salt	½ cup chopped walnuts (optional)
¾ teaspoon cinnamon	*Glaze (optional):*
½ teaspoon ginger	3 tablespoons maple syrup
2 eggs	1 teaspoon lemon juice
⅔ cup low-fat buttermilk, shaken	¼ -⅓ cup powdered sugar
½ cup pure maple syrup	

Preheat the oven to 350°F and coat a 9-inch square glass baking dish with cooking spray.

In a large bowl, combine the flours, baking soda, baking powder, salt, cinnamon, and ginger. Make a well in the center of the dry ingredients.

In another bowl, using a whisk beat the eggs to break up. Add the buttermilk, maple syrup, olive oil, molasses, and vanilla and maple extracts.

Pour the wet mixture into the well in the center of the dry. Stir until almost combined, then add the nuts, if using, and stir until completely moistened. Do not overmix.

Transfer the batter to the prepared pan and bake for 28–32 minutes or until a toothpick inserted into the center of cake comes out clean.

Cool in the pan on a wire rack.

Simple glaze for the cake (optional): Whisk the maple sugar, lemon juice, and powdered sugar together in a small bowl. Start with ¼ cup powdered sugar and add more as needed to achieve the desired consistency. Drizzle glaze on the cake just prior to serving.

Serves 9–12.

Peach Ginger Crisp

Fresh peaches are one of the delights of summer. Peel the peaches if you prefer, or leave the skins on for added color and vitamins.

Peach filling:

2½–3 lbs. peaches, pitted and sliced (about 6–8 peaches)

2 tablespoons peach schnapps or orange juice

¼ cup brown sugar

1 tablespoon cornstarch

Crisp topping:

½ cup all-purpose flour

½ cup whole wheat pastry flour

1¼ cups old-fashioned rolled oats

¼ teaspoon nutmeg

½ teaspoon cinnamon

¼ teaspoon salt

2 tablespoons minced crystallized ginger

⅓ cup olive oil

1 teaspoon vanilla extract

Preheat the oven to 350°F .

Combine all of the filling ingredients and mix. Transfer the mixture to an ungreased 11 x 9-inch glass baking dish.

In a medium bowl, combine flours, oats, nutmeg, cinnamon, salt, and ginger. Make a well in the center.

In a separate bowl, combine olive oil and vanilla. Pour the oil mixture into the center of the dry ingredients and rub with hands until a course meal forms.

Sprinkle the topping mixture over the peaches, distributing evenly. Bake for 45 minutes or until the top is light brown and the fruit bubbles.

Serve warm.

Makes 8 servings.

DAIRY FREE

Pumpkin Spice Cake with Cream Cheese Frosting

Simply delicious!

1½	cups plus 2 tablespoons all-purpose flour	1	teaspoon baking soda
1	cup granulated sugar	2	teaspoons cinnamon
½	cup brown sugar, packed	1	teaspoon ground ginger
¼	cup olive oil	½	teaspoon ground cloves
1	teaspoon vanilla extract	½	teaspoon salt
3	large eggs		*Frosting:*
1	(15-ounce) can unsweetened pumpkin (approx. 2 cups)	1	(8-ounce) package 33%-less-fat cream cheese, at room temperature
½	cup whole wheat pastry flour	3	cups powdered sugar
1	teaspoon baking powder	1	teaspoon vanilla extract

Preheat oven to 350°F. Coat two 8-inch round cake pans with cooking spray. Dust pans evenly with 2 tablespoons all-purpose flour. Knock out excess flour. Set aside.

In a large bowl combine granulated sugar, brown sugar, olive oil, and vanilla; beat with a mixer at medium speed for 2 minutes or until well blended. Add eggs, one at a time, beating well after each addition. Add pumpkin, beating until blended.

In a medium bowl combine 1½ cups all-purpose flour, pastry flour, baking powder, baking soda, spices, and salt. Gradually add flour mixture to pumpkin mixture, beating just until blended. Spoon batter into prepared pans.

Bake for 30 minutes or until a wooden toothpick inserted in center comes out clean. Cool in pans 10 minutes on a wire rack. Remove cake from pans; cool completely on wire rack.

To prepare the frosting: Beat cream cheese at medium speed until creamy. Gradually add powdered sugar and vanilla extract, beating until blended and light.

Place 1 cake layer on a serving plate. Spread 1 cup frosting over layer and top with remaining cake layer. Spread remaining frosting over top of cake.

Refrigerate any leftover cake.

Serves 14–16.

Rich Chocolate Fudge Cake

Right before serving, dust this cake with powdered sugar using a cake stencil. Make your own cake stencil by cutting a piece of stiff paper into a decorative shape and laying it on the top of the cake before dusting with powdered sugar. A small sieve works well for dusting.

½	cup unsweetened cocoa powder, sifted		1½	cups granulated sugar
½	cup brewed coffee, warm		⅓	cup olive oil
2	cups all-purpose flour		2	eggs
¼	teaspoon baking powder		2	teaspoons vanilla extract
1	teaspoon baking soda		1	cup low-fat buttermilk
½	teaspoon salt			

Preheat oven to 350°F and coat a 9 x 13-inch pan with cooking spray.

In a small bowl, combine cocoa powder and coffee; whisk until smooth. Set aside to cool.

Combine flour, baking powder, baking soda, and salt in another bowl.

In a large bowl, using a handheld mixer beat the sugar and olive oil. Add eggs, one at a time, beating after each egg until the mixture is light and fluffy. Mix in the cooled cocoa mixture, vanilla extract, and buttermilk.

Add the dry ingredients to the wet and beat about 2 minutes or until the mixture is smooth and well combined.

Pour the batter into the prepared pan and bake for 30 minutes or until a toothpick inserted into the center of the cake comes out clean.

Cool in the pan on a wire rack.

Makes 12 servings.

Spiced Raisin Cake

Reminiscent of Grandma's kitchen, this moist spice cake can be served as a dessert or as an addition to your brunch menu. And while it tastes sinful and rich, it isn't!

2	cups raisins	1	teaspoon instant coffee
1	cup brown sugar	2	teaspoons cinnamon
1¼	cups water	1	teaspoon salt
⅓	cup olive oil	1	teaspoon baking soda
1	teaspoon vanilla extract	1	teaspoon baking powder
1	tablespoon molasses	½	teaspoon cloves
1	cup all-purpose flour	½	teaspoon ginger
1	cup whole wheat pastry flour	½	teaspoon nutmeg

Mix raisins, brown sugar, and water in a saucepan. Heat to a boil while stirring. After the mixture reaches the boiling point, remove from the heat and allow to cool to room temperature. Add olive oil, vanilla, and molasses.

Preheat oven to 350°F. Lightly oil a 9 x 13-inch glass baking dish.

In a large bowl, combine all dry ingredients and spices. Make a well in the center of the dry ingredients and pour in raisin mixture. Stir just until combined.

Transfer batter to prepared baking dish. Bake for 35–40 minutes or until the top springs back when touched.

Cool and cut into 3 x 1-inch bars.

Store in an airtight container at room temperature for up to 1 week.

Makes 36 bars.

DAIRY-FREE

Surprise Apple Cake

Yes, cake with sauerkraut does work, but no, not on top of the cake! Chopped and mixed in the batter, the sauerkraut adds a healthy dose of vitamin C and a German/Polish twist to this delicious apple cake.

16 ounces sauerkraut, rinsed, squeezed dry, and finely chopped

1 large apple, peeled and coarsely grated (Granny Smith, Gravenstein, or Braeburn)

1 cup all-purpose flour

1 cup whole wheat pastry flour

2 teaspoons baking powder

1 teaspoon baking soda

1 teaspoon salt

2 teaspoons cinnamon

4 eggs

1 cup granulated sugar

½ cup brown sugar

2 teaspoons vanilla extract

¾ cup olive oil

1 cup chopped walnuts or pecans

Cream Cheese Frosting:

16 ounces low-fat or fat-free cream cheese

1 cup powdered sugar

2 tablespoons milk

2 teaspoons vanilla extract

1 teaspoon grated orange zest

Preheat the oven to 350°F and coat a 9 x 13-inch glass baking dish with cooking spray.

After rinsing and squeezing sauerkraut dry, place on a cutting board and chop to mince.

In a small bowl, combine the flours, baking powder, baking soda, salt, and cinnamon. Make a well in the center.

In a separate bowl, using a handheld mixer beat the eggs, granulated sugar, brown sugar, and vanilla extract until light and fluffy. Slowly add the olive oil with the mixer running and beat for another 2 minutes. Stir in grated apple, nuts, and sauerkraut.

Add the dry ingredients to the wet and stir just until well moistened.

Pour the batter into the prepared pan and bake for 40–50 minutes or until a toothpick inserted into the center of the cake comes out clean. Cool in the pan on a wire rack.

To make the frosting: Beat all of the frosting ingredients in a small bowl with a handheld mixer until smooth.

Serves 12–16.

DAIRY-FREE

Tropical Pineapple Upside-Down Cake

Delicious dessert—serve warm.

4	tablespoons olive oil, divided use	I	teaspoon baking powder
¾	cup light brown sugar, packed	¼	teaspoon salt
I	(15-ounce) can pineapple chunks in juice, drained, reserving juice	½	teaspoon cinnamon
		½	teaspoon ground ginger
I	cup flaked sweetened coconut	I	large egg
I	cup all-purpose flour	½	teaspoon vanilla extract
½	cup granulated sugar	½	cup mashed ripe banana
½	teaspoon baking soda		

Preheat oven to 375°F.

Using a 9-inch cast iron skillet, heat 2 tablespoons olive oil and swirl in pan to coat the bottom. Sprinkle brown sugar in the pan and cook until slightly bubbly. Remove from the heat and arrange well-drained pineapple chunks on the bottom of the pan in a single layer. Sprinkle with the coconut and set aside.

In a large bowl, combine flour, granulated sugar, baking soda, baking powder, salt, cinnamon, and ginger. In a separate bowl, whisk the egg slightly to break up, then add reserved pineapple juice, vanilla, mashed banana, and remaining 2 tablespoons olive oil; whisk again to mix wet ingredients.

Add the pineapple juice mixture to the dry ingredients and stir until well blended. Pour batter over the coconut/pineapple layer in the pan.

Bake for 30 minutes or until a wooden toothpick inserted into the center of the cake comes out clean. Cool in the pan on a wire rack for 15–20 minutes and then carefully invert the cake onto a large cake plate. Serve warm or at room temperature.

Serves 8–10.

DAIRY-FREE

CHAPTER 4
PANCAKES & WAFFLES

Apple Cinnamon Waffles

These waffles are even great frozen and then reheated. You are sure to discover many uses for left-over waffles. My family's favorite is to make sandwiches. Toast them and spread with natural peanut butter, or make a toasted waffle-cheese sandwich—what a treat! Add some thinly sliced apple to either of these sandwiches for a surprising crunch.

1	cup all-purpose flour	½	cup unsweetened applesauce
½	cup whole wheat pastry flour	1¼	cups low-fat buttermilk, shaken
1	tablespoon baking powder	2	tablespoons brown sugar
¼	teaspoon salt	1	teaspoon vanilla
1	teaspoon cinnamon	3	tablespoons olive oil
3	egg whites	¼	cup finely chopped walnuts (optional)
2	egg yolks		

Preheat waffle iron according to manufacturer's directions.

In a large bowl, whisk together flours, baking powder, salt, and cinnamon. Make a well in the center.

Using an electric mixer, beat the egg whites until soft peaks form. Set aside.

In another bowl, combine egg yolks, applesauce, buttermilk, brown sugar, vanilla, and olive oil. Using the mixer, beat until smooth.

Add the wet mixture (except the egg whites) to the dry and using the mixer again beat until well combined. Stir in walnuts, if using. Fold the egg whites into the batter gently.

Spray waffle iron with cooking spray and spoon ¾ cup to 1 cup of batter into iron. Cook according to the manufacturer's instructions or for about 5–6 minutes. Waffles will be light brown and slightly soft when done but will crisp up quickly.

Spray iron with cooking spray between batches.

Makes about 12 4″ waffles.

Apple Walnut Pancakes

No fruit plays a more prominent role in religion, myth, folklore, and literature than the humble apple. It symbolizes not only knowledge and wisdom, but also treachery and sin. From Mom and apple pie to the wicked witch and the poisoned apple, this fruit is a potent symbol of the complexity of human nature. Plus, it is delicious and healthy!

1 cup all-purpose flour	¼ cup olive oil
¾ cup whole wheat pastry flour	1 tablespoon brown sugar, packed
3 tablespoons wheat germ	1 cup low-fat milk
¼ teaspoon salt	1 teaspoon vanilla
2½ teaspoons baking powder	1 large apple, peeled and grated (about
1 teaspoon cinnamon	¾ cup grated)
3 egg whites	¼ cup chopped walnuts
2 egg yolks	

Preheat pancake griddle.

In a large bowl, combine flours, wheat germ, salt, baking powder, and cinnamon. Make a well in the center.

Using a handheld mixer, beat the egg whites until stiff but not dry. Set aside.

In a separate bowl, whisk together egg yolks, olive oil, brown sugar, milk, and vanilla. Stir in apple and walnuts.

Pour the wet ingredients into the dry and whisk until well blended and smooth. Stir in apple and walnuts. Gently fold in the egg whites until no egg whites are visible.

Use roughly ¼ cup batter per pancake.

Cook the pancakes until bottoms are golden brown and bubbles start to form on the top of the pancake, about 3 minutes. Using a spatula, flip the pancakes and continue cooking until bottoms are golden, about 2 more minutes.

Transfer to plates or keep warm in a 250°F oven in an ovenproof baking dish until ready to serve.

Makes about 12–14 small pancakes.

Apricot Waffles

These waffles remind me of the first time I ever tasted an apricot. It was at the holidays, and one of my aunts had sent a large box of dried fruit—the golden orange apricots spoke to me instantly. Since then, I have been a convert. They are naturally sweet and tangy, with a wonderful chewy texture—just right to satisfy any sweet tooth!

10	dried apricots, about ½ cup, chopped	3	eggs, separated
⅓	cup apricot preserves	¼	teaspoon salt
2	tablespoons lemon juice	1	cup low-fat or fat-free milk
1	cup all-purpose flour	½	cup low-fat buttermilk
1	cup whole wheat pastry flour	1	teaspoon vanilla extract
2	tablespoons wheat germ	½	teaspoon almond extract
1	tablespoon baking powder	¼	cup olive oil

Preheat waffle iron according to manufacturer's directions, usually around medium-high heat.

Place the apricots, apricot preserves, and the lemon juice in the bowl of a food processor. Process until the mixture is puréed.

In a large bowl, whisk together flours, wheat germ, baking powder, and salt. Make a well in the center.

In a medium bowl, beat the egg whites using a handheld mixer until soft peaks form. Set aside.

In another bowl, combine egg yolks, milk, buttermilk, apricot purée, vanilla and almond extracts, and olive oil. Using the mixer, beat until smooth.

Add the wet ingredients (except the egg whites) to the dry. Using the mixer, beat the batter until well combined. Fold the egg whites into the batter gently.

Spray waffle iron with cooking spray and spoon about ¾ cup to 1 cup of batter into iron. Cook about 5–6 minutes or according to the manufacturer's instructions. Waffles will be light brown and slightly soft when done.

Spray with cooking spray between batches.

Makes about 20 4″ waffles.

Cranberry Orange Waffles

These slightly tart waffles have a wonderful light and crisp texture. They are scrumptious with maple syrup or orange marmalade.

1	cup all-purpose flour		1	cup low-fat buttermilk, shaken
1	cup whole wheat pastry flour		1	teaspoon vanilla extract
1	tablespoon baking powder		¼	cup olive oil
¼	teaspoon salt		1	teaspoon orange zest, from one large orange
¼	teaspoon cinnamon		½	cup finely chopped cranberries (using food processor or by hand)
3	tablespoons sugar			
3	eggs, separated			
½	cup low-fat milk			

Preheat waffle iron according to manufacturer's directions.

In a large bowl, whisk together flours, baking powder, salt, cinnamon, and sugar. Make a well in the center.

Using an electric mixer, beat the egg whites until soft peaks form. Set aside.

In another bowl, combine egg yolks, milk, buttermilk, vanilla, olive oil, and orange zest. Using the mixer, beat until smooth.

Add the wet mixture to the dry (except the egg whites), and using the mixer again, beat until well combined. Fold the chopped cranberries and egg whites into the batter gently.

Spray waffle iron with cooking spray and spoon about ¾ cup to 1 cup of batter into iron. Cook according to the manufacturer's instructions or for about 6 minutes. Waffles will be light brown and slightly soft when done.

Spray with cooking spray between batches.

Makes about 20 4″ waffles.

Gingerbread Pancakes

These pancakes are dairy-free!

2	cups all-purpose flour		4	egg whites
1	cup whole wheat pastry flour		½	cup water
1	tablespoon baking powder		½	cup brewed coffee, at room temperature
1½	teaspoons baking soda		1	cup brown sugar
1	teaspoon salt		3	egg yolks
1½	teaspoons cinnamon		¼	cup fresh lemon juice
1½	teaspoons ginger		½	cup olive oil
¼	teaspoon ground cloves			

Preheat pancake griddle to medium hot.

In a large bowl, whisk together flours, baking powder, baking soda, salt, cinnamon, ginger, and cloves. Make a well in the center.

Using a handheld mixer beat the egg whites in a small bowl until soft peaks form. Set aside.

In another bowl, whisk together water, coffee, brown sugar, egg yolks, lemon juice, and olive oil.

Pour the wet ingredients (except the egg whites) into the well in the dry ingredients and beat using the handheld mixer until smooth, about 2 minutes. Gently fold in the egg whites.

Brush the griddle lightly with olive oil or spray with cooking spray. Spoon ¼ to ½ cup of batter per pancake on the griddle. Cook until golden brown, about 3 minutes, and then flip and continue cooking for another 2–3 minutes.

Serve warm.

Makes 20–24 pancakes.

DAIRY-FREE

Honey Whole Wheat Waffles

The combination of honey and whole wheat is perfect. Top these with jam or a combination of peanut butter and jam for a real treat!

1	cup all-purpose flour	½	teaspoon salt
1	cup whole wheat pastry flour	3	eggs, separated
¼	cup wheat germ	¼	cup honey
3	teaspoons baking powder	2	cups milk
½	teaspoon baking soda	¼	cup olive oil
1	tablespoon sugar		

Preheat waffle iron according to manufacturer's directions.

In a large bowl, whisk together flours, wheat germ, baking powder, baking soda, sugar, and salt. Make a well in the center.

Using an electric mixer, beat the egg whites until soft peaks form. Set aside.

In another bowl, combine egg yolks, honey, milk, and olive oil. Using the mixer, beat until smooth.

Add the wet mixture (except the egg whites) to the dry, and using the mixer again, beat until well combined. Gently fold the egg whites into the batter.

Spray waffle iron with cooking spray and spoon about ¾ cup to 1 cup of batter into iron. Cook about 5–6 minutes.

Be sure to spray iron with cooking spray between batches.

Makes about 12 4″ waffles.

Lemon Blueberry Waffles

These wonderful light, crisp waffles seem to add some sunshine and cheer to even the darkest, grayest mornings. The lemon flavor is clean and bright, with the blueberries adding the right amount of color and moisture.

1   cup all-purpose flour
1   cup whole wheat pastry flour
3   teaspoons baking powder
1   tablespoon granulated sugar
¼   teaspoon salt
3   eggs, separated
     Grated zest of one lemon (about 1–1½ teaspoons)

1½   cups milk
¼   cup fresh lemon juice
1   teaspoon vanilla extract
¼   cup olive oil
1½   cups fresh or frozen blueberries (if frozen allow to thaw)

Preheat waffle iron according to manufacturer's directions.

In a large bowl, whisk together flours, baking powder, sugar, and salt. Make a well in the center.

Using an electric mixer, beat the egg whites until soft peaks form. Set aside.

In another bowl, combine egg yolks, lemon zest, milk, lemon juice, vanilla, and olive oil. Using the mixer, beat until smooth.

Add the wet mixture to the dry and using the mixer again, beat until well combined. Gently fold the blueberries and egg whites into the batter.

Spray waffle iron with cooking spray and spoon about ¾ cup to 1 cup of batter into iron. Cook about 5–6 minutes or according to the manufacturer's instructions.

Be sure to spray the iron with cooking spray between batches.

Makes about 12 4″ waffles.

Mom's Best Pancakes

Dads, don't be intimidated—this is an easy-to-make crowd-pleaser. Beating the egg whites separately makes these flapjacks light and fluffy. Add fresh blueberries or raspberries and top with real maple syrup!

1½	cups all-purpose flour	1	teaspoon salt
1	cup whole wheat pastry flour	4	eggs, separated
2	tablespoons wheat germ	2	cups low-fat milk
1	tablespoon sugar	3	tablespoons olive oil
2½	teaspoons baking powder	1	teaspoon vanilla extract

Preheat pancake griddle.

In a large bowl combine flours, wheat germ, sugar, baking powder, and salt. Make a well in the center.

Using a handheld mixer, beat the egg whites until stiff but not dry. Set aside.

In a separate bowl, whisk together egg yolks, milk, olive oil, and vanilla.

Pour the wet ingredients (except the egg whites) into the dry and whisk until well blended and smooth. Gently fold in the egg whites until no egg whites are visible.

Use roughly ¼ cup batter per pancake.

Cook the pancakes until bottoms are golden brown and bubbles start to form on the top of the pancake, about 3 minutes. Using a spatula, flip the pancakes and continue cooking until bottoms are golden, about 2 more minutes.

Transfer to plates or keep warm in a 250°F oven on an ovenproof baking dish until ready to be served.

Makes about 20 medium pancakes; serves 6.

Paul Bunyan Banana Flapjacks

These hearty pancakes are sure to fill you up and keep you going all morning!

½	cup all-purpose flour	2	eggs, separated
½	cup whole wheat pastry flour	1	cup low-fat or fat-free milk
¼	cup wheat germ	2	tablespoons olive oil
1	tablespoon baking powder	1	teaspoon vanilla extract
1	tablespoon granulated sugar	2	large ripe bananas, halved lengthwise
½	cup quick or old-fashioned rolled oats		twice (to quarter) and then sliced thinly,
½	teaspoon cinnamon		about 1¼ cups
¼	teaspoon salt	¼	cup finely chopped walnuts or pecans

Preheat griddle.

In a large bowl, combine flours, wheat germ, baking powder, sugar, oats, cinnamon, and salt. Make a well in the center.

Using a handheld mixer, beat the egg whites until stiff but not dry. Set aside.

In a separate bowl, whisk together egg yolks, milk, olive oil, and vanilla.

Pour the wet ingredients (except the egg whites) into the dry and whisk until well blended and smooth. Stir in banana slices and nuts. Gently fold in the egg whites until no egg whites are visible.

Use roughly ¼ cup batter per pancake.

Cook the pancakes until bottoms are golden brown and bubbles start to form on the top of the pancake, about 3 minutes. Using a spatula, flip the pancakes and continue cooking until bottoms are golden, about 2 more minutes.

Transfer to plates or keep warm in a 250°F oven on an ovenproof baking dish until ready to serve.

Makes about 12–14 small pancakes.

Pumpkin Waffles

Pumpkin is one of my favorite ingredients. It makes cakes and cookies moist and flavorful, so why not waffles? Top them with sliced bananas, walnuts, and a touch of maple syrup. Great with apple butter, too!

1½	cups all-purpose flour	3	egg yolks
1	cup whole wheat pastry flour	1	cup low-fat milk
2½	teaspoons baking powder	1	cup low-fat buttermilk, shaken
½	teaspoon salt	1	cup canned pumpkin
2	teaspoons cinnamon	⅓	cup brown sugar
¼	teaspoon cloves	1	teaspoon vanilla extract
1	teaspoon ginger	⅓	cup olive oil
4	egg whites		

Preheat waffle iron according to manufacturer's directions.

In a large bowl, whisk together flours, baking powder, salt, cinnamon, cloves, and ginger. Make a well in the center.

Using an electric mixer, beat the egg whites until soft peaks form.

In another bowl, combine egg yolks, milk, buttermilk, pumpkin, brown sugar, vanilla, and olive oil. Using the mixer, beat until smooth.

Add the pumpkin mixture to the dry mixture, and using the mixer again, beat until well combined. Fold the egg whites into the batter gently.

Spray waffle iron with cooking spray and spoon about ¾ cup to 1 cup of batter into iron. Cook according to the manufacturer's instructions or for about 5–6 minutes. Waffles will be light brown and slightly soft when done, but will crisp up quickly.

Spray iron with cooking spray between batches.

Makes about 20 4″ waffles.

CHAPTER 5
QUICK BREADS

Apple Date Coffee Quick Bread

This might seem an unlikely combination—coffee, fruit, and nuts—but it works! The bread is moist and deeply flavored.

1 cup hot coffee (or 1 tablespoon instant coffee plus 1 cup boiling water)	½ teaspoon cinnamon
1⅓ cups (about 8 oz.) chopped dates	1 egg
1¼ cups all-purpose flour	¾ cup brown sugar
1 cup whole wheat pastry flour	2 tablespoons olive oil
2 teaspoons baking powder	1 teaspoon vanilla extract
½ teaspoon baking soda	1 cup peeled, grated apple
½ teaspoon salt	½ cup chopped walnuts

Preheat the oven to 350°F and coat one 9 x 5-inch loaf pan with cooking spray or use 3 mini loaf pans.

Dissolve the instant coffee in the boiling water. Pour hot coffee over the chopped dates. Set aside to cool.

In a large bowl, combine the flours, baking powder, baking soda, salt, and cinnamon. Make a well in the center.

In another large bowl, whisk together the egg, brown sugar, olive oil, and vanilla extract. Stir in the apples, walnuts, and the coffee-date mixture.

Pour the wet ingredients into the well in the center of the dry and stir just until moistened.

Transfer the batter to the prepared pans.

Bake for 60–65 minutes. If making mini loaves, bake for 40–50 minutes.

Cool in the pan on a wire rack for 10 minutes. Run a knife around the edge of the pan to loosen and remove, cooling completely on a wire rack.

Makes 1 large loaf or 3 mini loaves (10–12 servings).

DAIRY FREE

Applesauce Date Bread

Date palm trees have been cultivated in the Middle East for at least 6,000 years, primarily for their delicious fruit. We now know dates are high in many nutrients: fiber, phosphorus, iron, potassium, folate, vitamin A, and the B vitamins. Dates are beneficial for anemia, constipation, and fatigue. They are available year round and keep well, so eat more dates!

I	cup all-purpose flour	I	cup granulated sugar
I	cup whole wheat pastry flour	I	cup unsweetened applesauce
I	teaspoon baking soda	3	egg whites, lightly beaten
I	teaspoon baking powder	¼	cup olive oil
½	teaspoon salt	3	tablespoons low-fat buttermilk
I	teaspoon cinnamon	I	teaspoon vanilla extract
¼	teaspoon nutmeg	½	cup chopped walnuts or pecans
¼	teaspoon allspice	⅔	cup chopped dates

Preheat the oven to 350°F and coat a 9 x 5-inch loaf pan with cooking spray or oil.

In a large bowl, combine flours, baking soda, baking powder, salt, cinnamon, nutmeg, and allspice. Make a well in the center.

In another large bowl, combine sugar, applesauce, egg whites, olive oil, buttermilk, and vanilla. Whisk until well blended. Add the wet ingredients to the dry and stir just until moist. Do not overmix. Gently fold in nuts and dates.

Pour batter into prepared pan.

Bake for 60–65 minutes or until a toothpick inserted into the center of the loaf comes out clean.

Allow to cool in the pan for 10 minutes, then transfer to a wire rack to cool completely.

Makes I loaf (10–12 servings).

Blueberry Walnut Bread

Blueberries and walnuts are both power foods which you can make a part of your daily breakfast routine. Blueberries are now well-known as the food highest in antioxidants, while walnuts have one of the highest contents of omega-3 fatty acids. Both are powerful disease fighters.

1	cup all-purpose flour	1	egg
1	cup whole wheat pastry flour	2	tablespoons olive oil
⅔	cup granulated sugar	1	teaspoon vanilla extract
1½	teaspoons baking powder	1	teaspoon orange zest*
½	teaspoon baking soda	1	cup fresh or frozen blueberries (if frozen,
¼	teaspoon salt		thaw partially)
⅔	cup low-fat milk	¼	cup chopped walnuts

Preheat the oven to 350°F and coat an 8 x 4-inch loaf pan with cooking spray.

In a large bowl, combine the flours, sugar, baking powder, baking soda, and salt. Make a well in the center.

In another bowl, whisk together the milk, egg, olive oil, vanilla, and orange zest until well blended.

Pour the wet ingredients into the dry and stir with a few broad strokes, then add the blueberries and walnuts and continue stirring just until moistened.

Pour the batter into the prepared pan.

Bake for 55–60 minutes or until a toothpick inserted into the center of the loaf comes out clean.

Cool in the pan on a wire rack for 10 minutes. Run a knife around the edge of the pan to loosen and cool completely on a wire rack.

*Orange zest tip: If grating an orange for zest, wash well first.

Makes 1 loaf (10–12 servings).

Cherry Almond Mini Loaves

The alcohol cooks off, of course, but if you prefer an alcohol-free recipe you can replace the amaretto with an equal amount of orange juice and increase the amount of almond extract to 1½ teaspoons.

¾	cup finely chopped dried cherries (sweet or tart)	2	eggs
3	tablespoons amaretto liqueur	¼	cup brown sugar, packed
3	tablespoons water	¾	cup granulated sugar
1¼	cups all-purpose flour	1	teaspoon vanilla extract
1	cup whole wheat pastry flour	1	teaspoon almond extract
1	teaspoon baking soda	½	cup low-fat buttermilk, shaken
1	teaspoon baking powder	¼	cup olive oil
½	teaspoon salt	½	cup plus 2 tablespoons sliced or finely chopped almonds

In a small saucepan combine the cherries, amaretto, and water. Heat at low temperature until the cherries start to absorb some of the liqueur and the mixture becomes fragrant, about 4–5 minutes. Remove from heat and set aside to cool.

Preheat oven to 350°F. Coat three small 6 x 3 x 2-inch loaf pans with cooking spray or oil. (If you prefer to bake one large loaf, use a 9 x 5-inch pan and bake for 60–65 minutes or until a toothpick inserted into the center of the loaf comes out clean.)

In a small bowl, combine the flours, baking soda, baking powder, and salt.

In a large bowl, whisk together the eggs, sugars, and vanilla and almond extracts. Then add the buttermilk and olive oil. Add the cherries and any remaining liquid to the mixture.

Add the dry ingredients and using a large spoon stir briefly, then add ½ cup almonds and stir just until combined. Do not overmix.

Divide the batter among the prepared pans. Sprinkle remaining 2 tablespoons almonds over the loaves.

Bake for 35–40 minutes.

Cool for 5 minutes in the pan(s) on a wire rack. Round a knife around the edges and then invert to remove from the pans. Allow to cool completely on wire rack.

Makes 1 large loaf or 3 mini loaves (10–12 servings).

Carrot Applesauce Bread

During the growing season, head to your local farm stand or farmers' market to find the freshest, sweetest carrots for this recipe.

1½	cups all-purpose flour	3	cups grated carrots
¾	cup whole wheat pastry flour	¾	cup applesauce
⅔	cup granulated sugar	2	teaspoons vanilla extract
2	teaspoons baking soda	¼	cup olive oil
1	teaspoon salt	2	egg whites
2	teaspoons cinnamon	2	eggs
1	teaspoon nutmeg	1	cup chopped walnuts or pecans
½	teaspoon ground cloves	1	cup dried currants

Preheat the oven to 350°F and oil two 9 x 5-inch bread pans.

In a large bowl, combine flours, sugar, baking soda, salt, cinnamon, nutmeg, and cloves.

In a medium bowl, mix the carrots, applesauce, vanilla, olive oil, egg whites, and whole eggs.

Add the carrot mixture to the dry ingredients and stir just until combined. Gently stir in nuts and currants.

Divide batter between prepared pans.

Bake in the center of the oven for about 1 hour or until a toothpick inserted into the center of the loaf comes out clean.

Cool on a wire rack for 10 minutes and then remove from the pans to cool completely.

Makes 2 loaves.

DAIRY FREE

Italian Fruit and Nut Quick Bread

This dense, fruity cake is the perfect companion for afternoon tea. Have a tea party for eight or just one—either way this cake is reason alone to celebrate.

1½	cups unbleached all-purpose flour	¾	cup low-fat milk
1	cup whole wheat pastry flour	½	cup olive oil
2	teaspoons baking powder	½	cup raisins
1	teaspoon aniseed	¼	golden raisins
¼	teaspoon salt		Grated zest of 1 lemon
1	cup sugar		Grated zest of 1 orange
2	eggs, lightly beaten	⅓	cup pine nuts, divided

Preheat oven to 350°F.

In a large mixing bowl, stir together the flours, baking powder, aniseed, and salt. Stir in the sugar.

In a small bowl, whisk the eggs, milk, and olive oil together. Add to the dry ingredients and stir just until moist and blended. Add both kinds of raisins, lemon zest, orange zest, and half of the pine nuts and stir to distribute evenly.

Coat a loaf pan with cooking spray or a little olive oil. Transfer the batter into the pan and smooth the surface. Sprinkle the top with the remaining pine nuts.

Bake for 55 minutes or until a toothpick inserted in the center comes out clean. Let cool for 5 minutes on a wire rack. Remove from the pan and cool completely on a rack.

Makes 8 servings.

Pumpkin Streusel Bread

Pumpkin's deep orange pulp is loaded with Vitamin A and fiber, and is fat- and cholesterol-free. In addition to providing a variety of vitamins and minerals, pumpkin is the only fruit or vegetable to contain three different carotenoids (beta carotene, alpha carotene, and lutein) which protect against heart disease and cancer and may even help to slow the aging process.

Topping:

2	tablespoons brown sugar		¼	teaspoon nutmeg
1	tablespoon all-purpose flour		1	teaspoon cinnamon
½	teaspoon cinnamon		1	teaspoon ginger
1	tablespoon olive oil		¼	teaspoon allspice
			1	cup canned pumpkin
			½	cup olive oil
1	cup all-purpose flour		2	eggs, beaten
½	cup whole wheat pastry flour		¼	cup milk or water
½	teaspoon of salt		1	teaspoon vanilla extract
1	cup granulated sugar		½	cup chopped walnuts
1	teaspoon baking soda			

Preheat oven to 350°F and coat a 9 x 5-inch loaf pan with cooking spray or oil. In a small bowl, combine all four topping ingredients and rub together with fingers until crumbs form.

In a large bowl, whisk together the flours, salt, sugar, baking soda, nutmeg, cinnamon, ginger, and allspice.

In a separate bowl, mix the pumpkin, olive oil, eggs, milk, and vanilla. Add the dry ingredients and combine, but do not overmix.

Pour into prepared loaf pan. Sprinkle topping evenly over the surface of the loaf.

Bake for 50–60 minutes or until a toothpick inserted into the very center of the loaf comes out clean.

Let cool in the pan for 5 minutes and then remove and let cool on a rack.

Makes 1 large loaf.

Rich Chocolate Zucchini Bread

My daughter and I love to make this quick bread on a summer evening to enjoy the next day for dessert or an afternoon treat. While it is great fresh out of the oven, the flavor only gets better as it sits. Since the recipe makes two loaves, you can put one in the freezer to enjoy later.

1½ cups granulated sugar	⅔ cup unsweetened cocoa powder, sifted
3 eggs	1 teaspoon salt
½ cup olive oil	1 teaspoon baking soda
2 cups grated, packed zucchini	¼ teaspoon baking powder
½ cup applesauce	1½ teaspoons cinnamon
2 teaspoons vanilla extract	1 cup semisweet chocolate chips
1¾ cups all-purpose flour	⅔ cup chopped walnuts (optional)
1 cup whole wheat pastry flour	

Preheat oven to 350°F. Lightly oil two 9 x 5-inch loaf pans.

In a large bowl, combine sugar, eggs, and olive oil. Whisk until well mixed. Stir in zucchini, applesauce, and vanilla.

In another bowl, combine the flours, cocoa, salt, baking soda, baking powder, and cinnamon.

Add the flour mixture to the zucchini mixture and stir just until combined. Stir in chocolate chips and walnuts, if desired. Pour the batter into the prepared pans and bake for 55–65 minutes or until a toothpick inserted into the center of the loaf comes out clean.

Cool the breads in the pans on wire racks for 10 minutes. Run a knife around the edges of the pans to loosen and remove. Cool completely on wire rack.

Store at room temperature for up to 1 week. Wrap and freeze for up to 2 months.

Makes 2 loaves.

DAIRY-FREE

Zucchini Bread

This bread is an ideal housewarming gift—but it may be difficult to part with! Packed with zucchini, whole wheat flour, and only ⅓ cup of oil, it is guilt-free. Enjoy it for breakfast, a snack, or dessert. To use zucchini in any other way may just be a waste!

4	cups grated, packed zucchini	1	cup all-purpose flour
1½	teaspoons salt	1	cup whole wheat pastry flour
1⅓	cups granulated sugar	1	teaspoon baking soda
2	eggs	1	teaspoon baking powder
⅓	cup olive oil	2	teaspoons cinnamon
¼	cup vanilla or plain low-fat yogurt	¼	teaspoon ground cloves
1½	teaspoons vanilla extract	¼	teaspoon ground nutmeg

Toss the zucchini and salt in a large bowl and let sit for 15 minutes. Using a large slotted spoon, transfer the zucchini to a clean kitchen towel and wring out as much liquid as possible. Remove zucchini from the towel and set aside.

Preheat oven to 350°F. Lightly oil a 9 x 5-inch loaf pan.

In a large bowl, combine sugar, eggs, and olive oil. Whisk until well mixed. Stir in zucchini, yogurt, and vanilla.

In another bowl, combine the flours, baking soda, baking powder, cinnamon, cloves, and nutmeg.

Add the flour mixture to the zucchini mixture, and stir just until combined. Pour the batter into the prepared pan and bake for 55–65 minutes or until a toothpick inserted into the center of the loaf comes out clean.

Cool the bread in the pan on a wire rack for 10 minutes. Run a knife around the edges of the pan to loosen and remove. Cool completely on wire rack.

Store at room temperature for up to 1 week. Wrap and freeze for up to 2 months.

Makes 1 loaf.

CHAPTER 6
BROWNIES & BARS

Almond Banana Bars

The wild forms of the banana, the most popular tropical fruit, come from India and Malaysia. There are eighty-one different varieties used worldwide, but only five are grown commercially. The Cavendish is the "garden variety" found in supermarkets.

1 cup all-purpose flour	1 teaspoon almond extract
½ cup whole wheat pastry flour	½ cup olive oil
¾ cup wheat germ	2 eggs
2½ teaspoons baking powder	1½ cups ripe mashed bananas
1 teaspoon salt	1 cup whole almonds, toasted, cooled, and
1 cup low-fat buttermilk	finely chopped
1 cup brown sugar, packed	½ cup sliced almonds
1 teaspoon vanilla extract	

Preheat oven to 350°F and coat a 10 x 15-inch baking sheet with cooking spray.

In a large bowl, combine the flours, wheat germ, baking powder, and salt. Make a well in the center.

Using a whisk, blend the buttermilk, brown sugar, vanilla and almond extracts, olive oil, and eggs. Stir in the mashed banana.

Pour the wet ingredients into the well in the center of the dry and start to combine with a few broad stokes. Add the toasted, chopped almonds and continue to stir just until moistened.

Spread the batter into the prepared pan and sprinkle with sliced almonds.

Bake for 44–48 minutes or until a toothpick inserted into the center comes out clean.

Cool in the pan on a wire rack. Cut into bars.

Makes 36–48 bars.

Apricot Bars

Two thousand years ago a doctor named Tung Fung living in Luxian, China, started asking patients to plant apricots in his backyard instead of paying medical fees. According to legend, patients cured of serious illness planted five trees, and the rest planted one until eventually 100,000 apricot trees were planted. Apricot wood would become the symbol of the medical profession. The good doctor was onto something—not only are apricot trees beautiful, but the fruits are healthy and delicious.

1¼ cups old-fashioned rolled oats	2 tablespoons water
1 cup all-purpose flour	1 teaspoon vanilla extract
½ cup whole wheat pastry flour	*Filling:*
½ teaspoon salt	1 cup apricot preserves
½ teaspoon baking powder	1 cup finely chopped dried apricots (about
1 cup brown sugar, packed	6 oz.)
⅔ cup olive oil	½ cup chopped walnuts (optional)

Preheat oven to 375°F and coat a 9 x 13-inch glass baking dish with cooking spray or oil.

In a large bowl, combine the oats, flours, salt, and baking powder. Make a well in the center.

In another bowl, combine the brown sugar, olive oil, water, and vanilla extract. Whisk until blended.

Pour the wet ingredients into the dry and stir until well mixed. Reserve 1½ cups of this crumb mixture for the topping and press remainder into bottom of baking dish.

In a small bowl, combine the apricot preserves and chopped apricots. Evenly spread filling over bottom crust. Sprinkle reserved crumb topping (and chopped walnuts, if desired) over the filling.

Bake at 375°F for 25–30 minutes or until the top is lightly browned.

Allow to cool completely in the pan on a wire rack, then cut into bars.

Make 36–48 bars.

DAIRY-FREE **VEGAN**

Black Forest Brownies

This decadent, flavorful brownie is based on the traditional German Black Forest Torte. The combination of dried cherries and rich chocolate is out of this world! Cherries are high in vitamin A, while cocoa powder (especially the natural, non-alkalinized variety) is a good source of antioxidants.

1	cup all-purpose flour	½	teaspoon instant coffee granules
½	cup unsweetened cocoa powder, sifted	1½	teaspoons vanilla extract
½	teaspoon baking powder	⅓	cup olive oil
¼	teaspoon salt	⅔	cup finely chopped dried cherries
2	eggs	¼	cup chocolate chips
¾	cup granulated sugar	¼	cup semisweet mini chocolate chips
¼	cup brown sugar		

Preheat oven to 350°F and coat a 9-inch square glass baking dish with cooking spray.

In a small bowl, combine the flour, cocoa, baking powder, and salt.

In a large bowl, beat the eggs and granulated sugar with a handheld mixer, until light and fluffy. Add the brown sugar, coffee granules, and vanilla extract; beat for another 2 minutes. Add olive oil in a slow stream with the mixer running, beating for 2 more minutes.

Stir the dry ingredients into sugar-egg mixture. Add the dried cherries and ¼ cup chocolate chips and stir to evenly distribute.

Spread the batter into the prepared pan. Sprinkle with the mini chocolate chips.

Bake for 20–24 minutes or until the center of the brownies is slightly firm. Be careful not to overbake.

Cool in the pan on a wire rack, then cut.

Makes 16 brownies.

DAIRY-FREE

Caramel Apple Bars with Dates and Walnuts

So much more than a mere cookie bar, this scrumptious treat is a dessert not to be missed.

1	cup all-purpose flour	2	teaspoons vanilla extract
1	cup whole wheat pastry flour	2	tablespoons water
2	cups old-fashioned rolled oats		*Fruit filling:*
½	cup granulated sugar	1½	cups peeled, diced apple
½	cup brown sugar, packed	½	cup chopped walnuts
½	teaspoon baking soda	1	cup chopped dates
1	teaspoon cinnamon	1	cup low-fat caramel ice cream topping
½	teaspoon salt	3	tablespoons all-purpose flour
¾	cup olive oil		

Preheat oven to 350°F and spray a 9 x 13-inch glass baking dish with cooking spray.

In a large bowl, combine flours, oats, granulated sugar, brown sugar, baking soda, cinnamon, and salt. Make a well in the center. Add the olive oil, vanilla extract, and water. Blend well.

Reserve 1⅓ cups of crumb mixture in a small bowl. Press the remaining mixture into the bottom of the prepared pan. Bake crust for 15–17 minutes or until slightly puffed.

While the crust is baking, combine the apples, walnuts, dates, caramel topping, and 3 tablespoons flour. Stir until well mixed.

Distribute fruit mixture over the prepared crust. Sprinkle reserved crumb topping over fruit mixture and bake for another 25–30 minutes or until lightly browned.

Cool in the pan on a wire rack before cutting. Store in an airtight container.

Makes 54 bars.

DAIRY FREE

Chocolate Cherry Bars

Be sure to mince the cherries for this recipe so you are guaranteed a taste in every bite!

1	cup very finely chopped dried cherries	⅔	cup olive oil
¼	cup boiling water	3	tablespoons water
1¼	cups all-purpose flour	1	(8-ounce) package low-fat or fat-free
1½	cups old-fashioned rolled oats		cream cheese, room temperature
⅓	cup unsweetened cocoa powder, sifted	1	egg
½	teaspoon salt	1	teaspoon vanilla extract
½	teaspoon baking soda	2	tablespoons sugar
1	teaspoon vanilla extract		
1	cup brown sugar, packed		

Preheat oven to 375°F and coat a 9 x 13-inch glass baking dish with cooking spray.

In a small bowl, combine the chopped cherries and boiling water; set aside.

In a large bowl, combine the flour, oats, cocoa powder, salt, and baking soda. Make a well in the center.

Whisk together the vanilla extract, brown sugar, olive oil, and water. Add the wet ingredients to the dry and stir until well mixed. Reserve 1½ cups of this mixture for the topping. Press the remaining mixture into the prepared pan.

Drain the chopped cherries, but reserve the water in a small bowl.

Using a handheld mixer, beat the cream cheese, egg, vanilla, and sugar. Add the reserved water from the cherries and beat until smooth.

Spread the cream cheese mixture evenly on the prepared crust. Sprinkle with dried cherries and reserved crumb topping.

Bake for 25–30 minutes or until the top is lightly browned.

Allow to cool in the pan on a wire rack. Once completely cool, cut into bars.

Makes 36–48 bars.

Chocolate Raspberry Bars

It can be torture waiting to cut into these delicious smelling bars until they are completely cool. You will be rewarded for your patience, as the cooling time gives the flavors a chance to meld—and the texture of the bars will be slightly firmer.

1¼ cups all-purpose flour
1½ cups old-fashioned rolled oats
⅓ cup unsweetened cocoa powder, sifted
½ teaspoon salt
½ teaspoon baking soda
1 teaspoon vanilla extract
1 cup brown sugar, packed
⅔ cup olive oil

3 tablespoons water

Filling:

¼ cup granulated sugar
1 tablespoon cornstarch
2 cups raspberries, fresh or frozen, if frozen allow to thaw slightly
½ cup semisweet mini chocolate chips

Preheat oven to 375°F and coat a 9 x 13-inch glass baking dish with cooking spray.

In a large bowl, combine the flour, oats, cocoa powder, salt, and baking soda. Make a well in the center.

In a separate bowl, whisk together the vanilla, brown sugar, olive oil, and water.

Pour the wet ingredients into the dry and stir until well mixed. Reserve 1½ cups of this mixture for the topping. Press the remaining mixture into the prepared pan.

In a small bowl, combine the sugar, cornstarch, and raspberries. Evenly distribute the berries over the crust. Sprinkle with mini chocolate chips and reserved crumb topping.

Bake for 32–38 minutes or until the bars are set. The bars may look slightly underdone but will firm up as they cool.

Allow to cool in the pan on a wire rack. Once completely cool, cut into bars.

Makes 36–48 bars.

DAIRY-FREE VEGAN

Dark Chocolate Zucchini Brownies

The texture of these brownies is a cross between cake-like and chewy. The chocolate flavor shines through, however, and the zucchini is very subtle. Zucchini is available year-round in most produce departments, so don't wait for summer to try these!

1	cup all-purpose flour	1½	cups granulated sugar
1	cup whole wheat pastry flour	¾	cup olive oil
½	cup unsweetened cocoa powder, sifted	3	teaspoons vanilla extract
1½	teaspoons baking soda	1	teaspoon instant coffee crystals
1	teaspoon salt	⅓	cup chopped walnuts (optional)
2	cups zucchini, shredded		

Preheat oven to 350°F and spray a 9 x 13-inch glass baking dish with cooking spray.

In a medium bowl, whisk together flours, cocoa powder, baking soda, and salt. Set aside.

In a large bowl, combine the zucchini, sugar, olive oil, vanilla extract, and coffee crystals. Add the flour mixture and stir until well mixed. Stir in chopped walnuts, if desired.

Pour into the prepared pan and bake for 35–40 minutes.

Cool completely in pan on a wire rack and cut.

Makes 24 brownies.

DAIRY-FREE VEGAN

Decadent Coconut Bars

The combination of coconut and almonds in these bars is like a chewy macaroon with a thin cookie crust.

Crust:

½	cup brown sugar, packed
I	cup all-purpose flour
⅓	cup olive oil
2	teaspoons vanilla extract

Topping:

2	large eggs
I	cup brown sugar, packed
I	teaspoon vanilla extract
I	teaspoon almond extract
3	tablespoons all-purpose flour
½	teaspoon salt
I½	cups sweetened flaked coconut
I	cup finely chopped almonds

Preheat oven to 350°F.

In a medium bowl, mix together brown sugar, flour, olive oil, and vanilla extract until large crumbs form. Press this mixture into the bottom of a lightly oiled 9 x 13-inch glass baking dish. The crust will be very thin.

Bake for 12 minutes or until slightly puffed and lightly browned.

While the crust is baking, prepare the topping. In a medium bowl, whisk the eggs and sugar until smooth. Add vanilla and almond extracts, 3 tablespoons flour, and salt and whisk until smooth. Stir in coconut and chopped almonds.

Spread the topping over the prepared crust and smooth with a spatula. Bake for 20 minutes or until light brown.

Cut into squares right after removed from the oven. Cutting the bars before they cool will make the job much easier.

Cool in pan on wire rack.

Makes 48 bars.

DAIRY-FREE

Granola Bars

These healthy granola bars are a great alternative to run-of-the-mill varieties found in the supermarket cereal aisle. Customize them according to your tastes—if you love raisins, then use only raisins. Or add some figs or finely chopped apricots. If you prefer maple flavor, use ⅓ cup pure maple syrup in place of the honey. Minced, crystallized ginger adds a kick. The combinations are endless!

2	cups quick-cooking oats	½	cup honey
½	cup all-purpose flour	1	egg
½	cup whole wheat pastry flour	2	teaspoons vanilla extract
½	cup wheat germ	¼	cup raisins
½	teaspoon salt	¼	cup dried cranberries
1	teaspoon cinnamon	¼	cup chopped dates
¾	cup brown sugar, packed	½	cup walnuts, pecans, or peanuts
½	cup olive oil		

Preheat oven to 350°F and line a 9 x 13-inch baking dish with aluminum foil or parchment paper that has been sprayed with cooking spray.

In a large bowl, combine the oats, flours, wheat germ, salt, and cinnamon. Make a well in the center.

In a separate bowl, combine the brown sugar, olive oil, honey, egg, and vanilla extract. Whisk until smooth.

Add the wet ingredients to the dry and mix with a large spoon. Add the raisins, cranberries, dates, and nuts and mix until evenly distributed.

Press the mixture into the prepared pan. Bake for 25–30 minutes or until the edges are lightly browned.

Cool completely in the pan on a wire rack. To remove, invert the pan onto a cutting board and remove foil or parchment. Cut into bars.

Makes 12–16 bars.

DAIRY FREE

Lemon Bars

Much lighter than traditional lemon bars, these are given a health boost from whole wheat flour and almonds in the crust. They are a best-loved recipe in our household—as they will be in yours.

Crust:

1	cup whole wheat pastry flour
¼	cup granulated sugar
3	tablespoons almonds
	Pinch of salt
1	teaspoon freshly grated lemon peel
¼	cup buttermilk
2	tablespoons olive oil

Filling:

2	eggs
¾	cup granulated sugar
3	tablespoons fresh lemon juice
2	teaspoons freshly grated lemon peel
2	tablespoons all-purpose flour
	Powdered sugar

Preheat oven to 350°F. Lightly oil an 8 x 8 x 2-inch baking dish.

Place flour, sugar, almonds, salt, and lemon peel in the bowl of a food processor. Process until the nuts are ground to the size of coarse meal. Mix the buttermilk and olive oil in a small bowl. Incorporate the oil mixture into the dry ingredients using brief on-off motion of the processor, just until the crust starts to form into clumps.

Remove the crust mixture from the processor and press into the bottom of the prepared pan. Bake for 13–15 minutes or until lightly browned.

For the filling, blend the eggs, sugar, lemon juice, and lemon peel in a medium bowl, using a whisk. Once well mixed, whisk in the 2 tablespoons flour.

Pour the filling into the hot crust and continue baking for 20–22 minutes or until the bars are lightly browned and the filling is set.

Cool in the pan on a wire rack. Cut into bars, then dust lightly with powdered sugar.

Makes 20 bars.

Mincemeat Fruit Bars

Mincemeat can be an expensive ingredient. Consider buying an extra jar when it is on sale around Thanksgiving to have on hand to whip up a batch of these bars whenever the mood strikes. Or if you want to have some extra mincemeat for pie baking, try searching online for a mincemeat recipe that appeals to you. Traditional versions include beef or stock, but there are lots of all-fruit/vegetarian variations.

I cup whole wheat pastry flour	¼ cup milk
I cup all-purpose flour	I teaspoon vanilla extract
¾ cup granulated sugar	¼ cup brown sugar, packed
½ teaspoon salt	I (27-ounce) jar of mincemeat
½ cup olive oil	I cup chopped walnuts or pecans

Preheat oven to 400°F.

In a large bowl, combine the flours, granulated sugar, and salt. Set aside.

In another bowl, whisk together the olive oil, milk, vanilla extract, and brown sugar.

Add the wet ingredients to the dry and stir until the mixture is moist and crumbly.

Reserve I cup of the crumb mixture and firmly press the remainder into the bottom of a 9 x 13-inch glass baking dish. Top with an even layer of the mincemeat. Sprinkle with the nuts and then the reserved crumb mixture.

Bake for 30–32 minutes or until golden brown.

Allow to cool completely on a wire rack. Cut into bars.

Makes 40–48 bars.

Orange Cream Cheese Bars

1½	cups old-fashioned rolled oats		*Filling:*	
1	cup all purpose flour		4	tablespoons orange marmalade
½	cup whole wheat pastry flour		1½	teaspoons vanilla extract
½	teaspoon salt		1	tablespoon orange zest
½	teaspoon baking powder		1	egg
1	cup brown sugar, packed		2	tablespoons granulated sugar
⅔	cup olive oil		1	(8-ounce) package low-fat or fat-free
2	tablespoons water			cream cheese, room temperature
1	teaspoon vanilla extract		½	cup mini chocolate chips

Preheat oven to 375°F and coat a 9 x 13-inch glass baking dish with cooking spray.

In a large bowl, combine the oats, flours, salt, and baking powder. Make a well in the center.

In another bowl combine the brown sugar, olive oil, water, and 1 teaspoon vanilla extract. Whisk until blended.

Pour the wet ingredients into the dry and stir until well mixed. Reserve 1½ cups of this mixture for the topping. Press the remaining mixture into the prepared pan.

Using a handheld mixer, beat the marmalade, 1½ teaspoons vanilla extract, orange zest, egg, sugar, and cream cheese until smooth. Spread the filling over the prepared crust.

Sprinkle mini chocolate chips and reserved crust over the filling.

Bake for 25–30 minutes or until the top is lightly browned.

Allow to cool in the pan on a wire rack before cutting into bars.

Makes 36–48 bars.

Peanut Butter Toffee Bars

1	cup old-fashioned rolled oats	⅔	cup chunky-style natural peanut butter
1	cup all-purpose flour	1	egg
½	cup whole wheat pastry flour	2	teaspoons vanilla extract
1	teaspoon baking soda	1	tablespoon water
¼	teaspoon salt	1	cup toffee bits or crushed chocolate-covered toffee candy bars
1	cup brown sugar, firmly packed		
⅓	cup olive oil		

Preheat oven to 375°F and coat a 9 x 13-inch glass baking dish with cooking spray or oil.

In a small bowl, combine oats, flours, baking soda, and salt.

Using a handheld mixer, combine brown sugar, olive oil, peanut butter, egg, vanilla extract, and water. Beat until smooth.

With a large spoon, stir the dry ingredients into the wet until well combined.

Press the dough into the prepared pan and top with the toffee bits.

Bake for 15 minutes or until light brown and puffed looking.

Cool on a wire rack and cut into bars. Store in an airtight container.

Makes 36 bars.

DAIRY-FREE

Peppermint Brownies

This cake-like brownie is ideal with a scoop of low-fat ice cream or frozen yogurt. If you would prefer something a bit more decadent, let the brownies cool for 5 minutes and then sprinkle with ½ cup chocolate chips. Once they have melted, spread the chocolate evenly on the top and sprinkle with crushed peppermint candies or candy canes.

⅓	cup chocolate chips	1	teaspoon instant coffee crystals
5	tablespoons olive oil	1	cup sugar
1	cup all-purpose flour	2	eggs
½	cup unsweetened cocoa powder, sifted (not Dutch process)	1	teaspoon vanilla extract
		½	teaspoon mint extract
¼	teaspoon baking soda	¼	cup low-fat buttermilk
¼	teaspoon salt		

Preheat oven to 350°F and coat an 8-inch square glass baking dish with cooking spray.

In a small microwave-proof bowl, combine chocolate chips and olive oil. Microwave on high at 15 second intervals. Stir and heat until smooth and chocolate is completely melted. Set aside to cool.

In another bowl, combine the flour, cocoa powder, baking soda, salt, and coffee crystals.

In a large bowl, combine the sugar, eggs, and vanilla and mint extracts, and whisk until smooth. Add buttermilk and cooled oil/chocolate chip mixture. Whisk until smooth.

Add the dry ingredients to the wet and stir just until moist. Spread the batter into the prepared pan.

Bake for 24–28 minutes or until a toothpick inserted into the center comes out clean.

Cool on a wire rack.

Makes 12 brownies.

Raspberry Oat Bars

If you are a raspberry lover, don't overlook these bars.

½ cup old-fashioned rolled oats
1 cup all-purpose flour
½ cup whole wheat pastry flour
½ teaspoon salt
½ teaspoon baking powder
1 cup brown sugar, packed
⅔ cup olive oil
2 tablespoons water

1 teaspoon vanilla extract
1 teaspoon almond extract
½ cup sliced almonds
Filling:
¼ cup granulated sugar
1 tablespoon cornstarch
2 cups raspberries, fresh or frozen (if frozen allow to thaw slightly)

Preheat oven to 375°F and coat a 9 x 13-inch glass baking dish with cooking spray.

In a large bowl, combine the oats, flours, salt, and baking powder. Make a well in the center.

In another bowl, combine the brown sugar, olive oil, water, and vanilla and almond extracts. Whisk until blended.

Pour the wet ingredients into the dry and stir until well mixed. Reserve 1½ cups of this mixture for the topping. Press the remaining mixture into the prepared pan.

Mix reserved crust and sliced almonds. Set aside.

In a small bowl, combine the sugar, cornstarch, and raspberries. Evenly distribute the berry mixture over the crust. Sprinkle reserved crust and almond mixture over the berries.

Bake for 25–30 minutes or until the top is lightly browned. The bars will look slightly underdone but will firm up as they cool.

Allow to cool in the pan on a wire rack. Once completely cool, cut into bars.

Makes 36–48 bars.

DAIRY-FREE

Sinful Raspberry Brownies

Really, these incredible brownies are wickedly good—and maybe a bit good for you. Chocolate is known to boost mood and has antioxidant benefits, so enjoy without guilt!

¾ cup all-purpose flour	1 tablespoon raspberry liqueur (such as Chombard) or water
¼ teaspoon baking powder	
¼ teaspoon baking soda	1 teaspoon vanilla extract
⅛ teaspoon salt	2 large eggs
1 cup sugar	3 tablespoons seedless raspberry preserves, stirred to loosen
⅔ cup unsweetened cocoa powder, sifted	
¼ cup olive oil	⅓ cup semisweet chocolate chips

Preheat oven to 350°F. Spray only the bottom of an 8-inch square glass baking dish with cooking spray.

In a medium bowl, combine the flour, baking powder, baking soda, and salt.

In a separate bowl, combine sugar, cocoa, olive oil, raspberry liqueur, vanilla extract, and eggs; stirring well with a whisk. Add the cocoa mixture to the flour mixture, stirring just until moist.

Pour batter into prepared dish, spreading evenly. Drop preserves by the scant teaspoonful onto the batter, and using the blade of a butter knife, swirl the jam into the batter. Sprinkle with chocolate chips.

Bake for 40 minutes or until a toothpick inserted in center comes out almost clean. Cool on a wire rack.

Makes 12–16 brownies.

DAIRY-FREE

CHAPTER 7

COOKIES & BISCOTTI

Almond and Hazelnut Biscotti

You are sure to get a delightful crunch of nuts in every bite of these classic biscotti. Toasting the almonds and hazelnuts helps to release their flavor.

3	cups all-purpose flour	I	teaspoon vanilla extract
I½	cups whole wheat pastry flour	I	teaspoon almond extract
I	teaspoon baking powder	5	large eggs
¾	teaspoon salt	I	tablespoon fresh orange zest
I	teaspoon cinnamon	I½	cups almonds, toasted and chopped
I¼	cups granulated sugar	I	cup hazelnuts, toasted, skins removed and
¼	cup olive oil		chopped coarsely

Preheat oven to 350°F. Lightly oil and flour two large cookie sheets.

In a medium bowl, combine flours, baking powder, salt, and cinnamon.

In a large bowl, whisk together sugar, olive oil, vanilla and almond extracts, eggs, and orange zest.

Stir the dry mixture into the wet until well combined, then stir in the almonds and hazelnuts.

Turn the dough out onto a floured board and knead several times. Divide into 4 equal portions, shaping each into a rectangle roughly 9 x 3 inches. Pat rectangles out slightly, to approximately 11 x 4 inches. Transfer to lightly oiled and floured pans, leaving about 3 inches between rectangles.

Bake for 25–30 minutes. Remove from oven and allow to cool for 5 minutes. Reduce oven temperature from 350°F to 325°F.

Remove logs to cutting surface. Using a serrated knife, create the biscotti by cutting at a slight diagonal across the logs, making ½- to ¾-inch slices (15–20).

Lay cookies cut-side down on the cookie sheets and bake at 325°F for 20 minutes. Remove the cookies from the oven, turn over, and bake for an additional 15 minutes on the other side.

Transfer the biscotti to a wire rack and cool completely. Store the biscotti in an airtight container for up to 3 weeks.

Makes 5 dozen biscotti.

DAIRY-FREE

Almond Aniseed Cookies

Anise is one of the oldest cultivated spices. In first-century Rome, anise was used in a popular spice cake served after a feast as a digestive aid. With its sweet licorice taste, anise is a favorite in Italian baking.

2	cups all-purpose flour	½	teaspoon vanilla extract
I	cup whole wheat pastry flour	I	cup granulated sugar
2	teaspoons baking powder	¼	cup olive oil
¼	teaspoon salt	I½	teaspoons aniseed, bruised if whole*
2	eggs	I	cup almonds, toasted and chopped
2	egg whites		

In a small bowl, combine flours, baking powder, and salt.

In a large bowl, combine eggs, egg whites, vanilla extract, and sugar; beat with a handheld mixer until light and slightly thickened. Add olive oil and aniseed and stir to combine.

Stir in the flour mixture, then add the nuts and stir to thoroughly mix. Dough will be sticky.

Cover and refrigerate the dough for a minimum of 2 hours.

Once the dough has cooled, preheat oven to 350°F. Line two baking sheets with parchment paper.

Turn the dough onto a lightly floured surface, divide, and shape into 2 round logs, each 15 inches long. Place logs on parchment-lined baking sheets and bake for 30 minutes.

Remove cookie logs from oven, but maintain oven temperature. Remove to a wire rack to cool for 5 minutes.

Using a serrated knife, slice the cookie logs into ½-inch-thick slices and place cookies on the parchment-lined baking sheets. Bake at 350°F for 20 minutes. Remove the cookies from the oven, turn over, and bake for an additional 15 minutes on the other side.

Cool completely on wire rack. Store in an airtight container for up to 3 weeks.

*Note: If using whole aniseeds, use a mortar and pestle or other heavy, blunt tool to bruise them prior to adding to the dough.

Makes 4 dozen cookies.

DAIRY FREE

Almond Thumbprint Cookies

These flavorful cookies are simple and delicious. Use any kind of jam or preserves. They are great with flavorful marmalades, especially apricot.

I	cup almonds	½	cup olive oil
I	cup old-fashioned rolled oats	I½	teaspoons vanilla extract
I	cup plus 2 tablespoons whole wheat pastry flour	I	teaspoon almond extract
¼	teaspoon salt	½	cup jam of your choice (e.g., raspberry, apricot, strawberry, grape)
½	cup maple syrup		

Preheat oven to 350°F.

Mix the almonds and oats in a food processor or blender and grind until the consistency of fine crumbs.

In a large bowl, combine the almond/oat mixture, wheat flour, and salt. In a small bowl, whisk the maple syrup, olive oil, and vanilla and almond extracts. Then add to the dry ingredients and stir until a thick dough forms.

Divide and roll the dough into I¼-inch balls and place on baking sheets. Make a depression in the center of each ball with thumb. Mend any cracks that develop in the sides of the cookie.

Fill the center of the cookie with about ½ teaspoon jam. Do not overfill.

Bake cookies for I5–20 minutes or until lightly browned.

Transfer to a wire rack to cool.

Makes 2–3 dozen cookies.

DAIRY-FREE

Apple Butter Cookies

These cookies are like a chewy, spicy oatmeal cookie. The outside is slightly crisp and the inside is soft. Purchased apple butter is good, but homemade apple butter makes these delicious cookies even better.

½	cup all-purpose flour	I	egg
½	cup whole wheat pastry flour	I	cup brown sugar, packed
¾	cup quick-cooking oats	¼	cup olive oil
I	teaspoon cinnamon	½	cup apple butter (recipe on page 84)
½	teaspoon baking powder	½	cup chopped walnuts
½	teaspoon baking soda	½	cup currants or raisins
½	teaspoon salt		

In a medium bowl, combine the flours, oats, cinnamon, baking powder, baking soda, and salt.

In a large bowl, combine the egg and brown sugar and beat using a handheld mixer. Add the olive oil and beat until the mixture is light and fluffy. Stir in the apple butter.

Add the dry ingredients to the wet and stir just until combined. Stir in the walnuts and currants or raisins.

Chill the cookie dough for at least I hour.

Preheat oven to 350°F. Line two baking sheets with parchment paper.

Drop the chilled cookie dough by rounded spoonfuls onto the parchment-lined baking sheets.

Bake for 13–15 minutes or until the edges of the cookies are slightly brown.

Allow to cool on the pans for 5 minutes. Transfer to a wire rack to cool completely.

Makes 3 dozen cookies.

DAIRY-FREE

Grandma's Apple Butter

Apple butter is a lovely spread for bread or crackers and as a dip for fruits. I enjoy it stirred into hot oatmeal in the winter. The flavor of homemade apple butter surpasses the commercially produced products usually found in the supermarket.

15	medium apples, roughly 4–5 pounds (Macintosh or Cortland is a great choice)	¾	teaspoon ground allspice
		¼	teaspoon ground cloves
3	cups apple cider (or juice)	½	cup light brown sugar
2	teaspoons ground cinnamon	1½	cups granulated sugar

Wash, core, and quarter apples. You can leave the peels on.

Place the apples in a large kettle or Dutch oven along with the cider or juice. Bring to a simmer. Cover and continue to simmer for about 30 minutes, making sure to stir occasionally to prevent sticking.

Remove from heat and press the mixture through a sieve or food mill. Return processed apples to the Dutch oven. Stir in the cinnamon, allspice, cloves, and sugars.

Bring to a bare simmer and reduce heat. Leave uncovered and cook over very low heat for about 1½ hours, until mixture is very thick. Be sure to stir periodically and frequently to prevent burning on the bottom.

Spoon finished apple butter into hot, sterilized canning jars—half pints are a perfect choice. Leave ¼ inch of head space. Wipe rims clean and close with lids and rings. Allow jars to cool on the counter before refrigerating.

Keep 1 month in the refrigerator or freeze for up to 4 months.

Makes 8 cups.

Applesauce Cookies

Children just love these cookies! Bake a batch of these on a crisp fall afternoon to fill the house with the delicious aroma of spices, and watch everyone come running.

½	cup all-purpose flour	½	teaspoon salt
½	cup whole wheat pastry flour	I	cup unsweetened applesauce
I	cup quick-cooking oats	⅓	cup olive oil
I	teaspoon baking soda	I	teaspoon vanilla extract
I½	teaspoons cinnamon	2	eggs
¼	teaspoon nutmeg	½	cup raisins or currants
¼	teaspoon ground cloves	½	cup chopped walnuts
½	teaspoon allspice		

Preheat oven to 375°F and line two baking sheets with parchment paper.

In a large bowl, combine flours, oats, baking soda, cinnamon, nutmeg, cloves, allspice, and salt. Make a well in the center.

In a medium bowl, whisk together applesauce, olive oil, vanilla extract, and eggs.

Pour wet ingredients into the dry and stir just until moist. Gently fold in the raisins or currants and walnuts.

Drop by rounded spoonfuls onto prepared baking sheet.

Bake for 10–12 minutes. Allow to cool for a few minutes on the baking sheets, and then transfer to a wire rack to cool completely.

Makes about 3 dozen cookies.

DAIRY FREE

Apricot Almond Chews

These cookies are the perfect balance of almond and apricot—a marriage made in heaven. They are a chewy cookie that freezes really well. Allow them to come up to room temperature and enjoy!

¾	cup all-purpose flour		I	egg
½	cup whole wheat pastry flour		¾	cup granulated sugar
I	teaspoon baking soda		¼	cup brown sugar
½	teaspoon salt		I	tablespoon water
⅓	cup olive oil		¾	cup diced dried apricots
I	teaspoon vanilla extract		¾	cup chopped raw almonds
½	teaspoon almond extract			

Preheat oven to 350°F and line a baking sheet with parchment paper.

In a small bowl, combine the flours, baking soda, and salt.

In a large bowl, whisk together the olive oil, vanilla and almond extracts, egg, sugars, and water. Add the dry ingredients to the wet and stir until well combined. Add the apricots and almonds and stir.

Drop by rounded spoonfuls onto the prepared baking sheet. Bake one pan of cookies at a time.

Bake for 10–12 minutes or until slightly brown at the edges. Allow to cool on the pans for 5 minutes, then transfer to a wire rack to cool completely.

Makes 3 dozen cookies.

DAIRY-FREE

Chocolate Brownie Cookies

Save these decadent cookies for a special occasion!

1	cup semisweet chocolate chips	1½	teaspoons baking powder
3	ounces unsweetened chocolate, chopped	3	eggs
⅓	cup olive oil	1	cup granulated sugar
1	cup all-purpose flour	2	tablespoons instant coffee granules
¼	cup whole wheat pastry flour	1	tablespoon vanilla extract
½	teaspoon salt	1	cup chopped walnuts

Preheat oven to 350°F and line two baking sheets with parchment paper.

In a small microwavable bowl, combine the semisweet chocolate chips, unsweetened chocolate, and olive oil. Microwave for 30 seconds at medium power, stir and repeat until the mixture is smooth. Take care not to overheat the mixture. Set aside to cool.

In a small bowl, whisk together the flours, salt, and baking powder.

In a large bowl, combine the eggs, sugar, instant coffee crystals, and vanilla extract. Using a handheld mixer, beat until light and fluffy. With the mixer running, add the cooled chocolate mixture and beat until well combined.

Add the dry ingredients to the chocolate-egg mixture and stir by hand until almost combined. Add the walnuts and stir until blended. Dough will be very fudgy and thick.

Drop by rounded teaspoonfuls onto the baking sheet.

Bake for 9–10 minutes. These chocolaty cookies will look slightly underdone when cooked; take care not to overbake.

Makes 4 dozen cookies.

DAIRY-FREE

Chocolate Crinkles

While these chocolaty cookies look impressive, they are easy to make. Serve them warm with milk!

4	1-oz. squares unsweetened chocolate, melted and cooled	3	eggs
1	cup all-purpose flour	1½	cups granulated sugar
1	cup whole wheat pastry flour	½	cup olive oil
2	teaspoons baking powder	¼	cup milk
¼	teaspoon salt	2	teaspoons vanilla extract
		1	cup powdered sugar

To melt chocolate: Chop up chocolate squares and place in a small glass bowl. Microwave at medium power for 30 seconds. Stir and repeat until chocolate is melted. You can also use the double boiler method: set a small metal bowl filled with the chopped chocolate over a pan of barely simmering water and stir chocolate until melted.

In a small bowl, combine the flours, baking powder, and salt.

In a large bowl, beat eggs and granulated sugar with a handheld mixer until light, then add olive oil and continue to mix until incorporated. Add melted chocolate, milk, and vanilla extract to mixture and beat until well-mixed.

Using a large spoon, stir dry ingredients into wet until incorporated.

Chill cookie dough overnight or 4 hours minimum.

Preheat oven to 375°F and line two baking sheets with parchment paper.

Using 1 teaspoon of dough, shape into ball using your hands and roll dough ball in powdered sugar to coat.

Place dough balls on a cookie sheet and bake for 12–14 minutes. Allow to cool for 2 minutes on the pan and then transfer to a wire rack to cool.

Makes 4 dozen cookies.

Classic Chocolate Chippers

These are a family favorite. They are crisp cookie with a light flavor reminiscent of a sugar cookie. Add raisins or other dried fruit. Also great with one teaspoon of cinnamon added.

1½	cups all-purpose flour	1	cup granulated sugar
1	cup whole wheat pastry flour	¾	cup olive oil
1	teaspoon salt	3	teaspoons vanilla extract
1	teaspoon baking soda	1½	cups chocolate chips
2	eggs	½	cup chopped walnuts (optional)
½	cup brown sugar, packed		

Preheat oven to 350°F.

In a small bowl, combine the flours, salt, and baking soda.

In a large bowl, combine the eggs and sugars and beat using a handheld mixer, until light and fluffy. Then add the olive oil and vanilla extract and continue to beat for another 2 minutes.

Add the dry ingredients to the wet and stir until combined. Add the chocolate chips and walnuts, if using.

Drop the dough by rounded spoonfuls onto baking sheets, about 3 inches a part.

Bake for 14–16 minutes or until lightly browned. Allow cookies to cool 2 minutes on pans, then transfer to wire racks to cool completely.

Makes 4 dozen cookies.

DAIRY FREE

Cinnamon Date Cookies

My grandmother made incredible cookies. These cookies remind me of trips to her house and the distinctive rattle of the cookie jar lid. For this recipe, be sure to use the chopped dates that are lightly coated with sugar.

1½	cups all-purpose flour	1	cup granulated sugar
1	cup whole wheat pastry flour	½	cup unsweetened applesauce
1	teaspoon baking powder	1	tablespoon water
½	teaspoon baking soda	2	teaspoons vanilla extract
½	teaspoon salt	¾	cup dried chopped dates
¼	teaspoon ground ginger		*Topping:*
½	teaspoon ground cinnamon	¼	cup granulated sugar
⅓	cup olive oil	1	teaspoon cinnamon

In a large bowl, combine flours, baking powder, baking soda, salt, ginger, and ½ teaspoon cinnamon. Make a well in the center.

In a separate bowl, whisk together olive oil, granulated sugar, applesauce, water, and vanilla extract. Stir in dates, first breaking up any clumps.

Pour the wet ingredients into the dry and stir until well combined. Cover and refrigerate a minimum of 2 hours, or up to 2 days.

Preheat oven to 350°F. Line two baking sheets with parchment paper.

To make the topping: In a small bowl, combine ¼ cup sugar and 1 teaspoon cinnamon.

Roll cookie dough into 1- to 1½-inch balls. Roll these in prepared cinnamon sugar. Place on prepared baking sheets 3 inches apart.

Bake for 14–16 minutes or until very lightly browned. Cool on the pans for 5 minutes and then transfer to a wire rack to cool completely.

Makes 3 dozen cookies.

DAIRY-FREE

Cranberry Orange Cookies

The aroma of these cookies takes me back to holidays when I was a child; our house was a cookie factory! My mother would make dozens of cookies for friends and neighbors. There is nothing more wonderful or more appreciated than a gift from your kitchen.

1½   cups quick-cooking oats
¾   cup whole wheat pastry flour
¾   cup all-purpose flour
1   teaspoon baking powder
½   teaspoon salt
½   cup honey
½   cup olive oil

2   teaspoons vanilla extract
½   cup orange juice
1   tablespoon grated orange zest, from one large orange
¾   cup dried cranberries
¾   cup sliced almonds

Preheat oven to 350°F and line two baking sheets with parchment paper.

In a medium bowl, combine the oats, flours, baking powder, and salt.

In a large bowl, using a whisk, combine the honey, olive oil, vanilla extract, orange juice, and orange zest. Add the dry ingredients and stir until moistened. Stir in the cranberries and almonds.

Drop by rounded tablespoonfuls onto prepared baking sheets. Flatten the cookie slightly with the back of a spoon to a thickness of about ½ inch.

Bake for 12–14 minutes or until slightly browned. Transfer to a wire rack to cool completely.

Makes 3 dozen cookies.

DAIRY-FREE

Double Chocolate Espresso Biscotti

Imagine yourself sitting at a sidewalk café in Florence or Rome, your only company a cup of fragrant coffee and one of these richly flavored cookies. That café experience is as close as your kitchen. . . .

1½	cups all-purpose flour	¼	cup olive oil
¼	cup unsweetened cocoa powder, sifted	½	cup sugar
1½	teaspoons baking powder	2	large eggs
½	teaspoon salt	2	teaspoons vanilla extract
2	tablespoons espresso powder (or instant coffee crystals)	½	cup mini chocolate chips
2	tablespoons low-fat milk		

Preheat oven to 350°F. Line a large baking sheet with parchment paper.

In a small bowl, combine the flour, cocoa powder, baking powder, and salt.

In another bowl, dissolve the espresso (or instant coffee) in the milk.

In a large bowl, whisk olive oil and sugar until well mixed. Add eggs, one at a time, beating well after each. Add vanilla extract and coffee-milk mixture.

With a large spoon, stir the flour mixture into the wet ingredients. Mix in the mini chocolate chips.

Turn out dough onto a lightly floured work surface and divide in half. Shape each half into a 10 x 4-inch rectangular log. Place the logs about 2 inches apart on the prepared baking sheet.

Bake the log in the center of the oven until puffed and golden, about 25–30 minutes. Remove from oven and let cool on a wire rack for 10 minutes. Leave the oven on.

Place the logs on a clean cutting surface. With a serrated knife, create the biscotti by cutting at a slight diagonal across the logs, making ½- to ¾-inch slices (15–20 pieces).

Lay cookies cut-side down on the parchment-lined cookie sheets and bake for 15 minutes. Remove the cookies from the oven, turn over, and bake for an additional 10 minutes on the other side.

Transfer the biscotti to a wire rack and cool completely. Store the biscotti in an airtight container for up to 3 weeks.

Makes 3 dozen biscotti.

Explosion Cookies

Loaded with fruit, nuts, and seeds, each bite of these cookies is different. They are a virtual taste explosion!

½	cup finely chopped dried apricots	½	teaspoon salt
¼	cup raisins	I	teaspoon baking soda
¼	cup dried cranberries	I	egg
½	cup chopped dates	I	teaspoon vanilla extract
¾	cup orange juice concentrate	½	cup olive oil
I½	cups old-fashioned rolled oats	¼	sunflower seeds
½	cup all-purpose flour	¼	cup sesame seeds
½	cup whole wheat pastry flour	¼	cup chopped walnuts

In a saucepan combine the apricots, raisins, cranberries, dates, and the orange juice concentrate. Simmer on low heat for 10 minutes. Set aside to cool.

Preheat oven to 350°F and line a baking sheet with parchment paper.

In a large bowl, combine the oats, flours, salt, and baking soda. Make a well in the center.

In another bowl, whisk together the egg, vanilla extract, and olive oil. Pour oil mixture and the cooled fruit mixture into the bowl with the dry ingredients and stir to combine. Stir in the sunflower seeds, sesame seeds, and walnuts.

Drop the cookie dough by rounded spoonfuls onto the prepared baking sheets. Flatten to a thickness of ¼ inch.

Bake for 12–15 minutes or until lightly browned. Cool on the pan for 5 minutes, then transfer to a wire rack to cool completely.

Makes 2 dozen cookies.

DAIRY FREE

Good Seed Cookies

These are my husband's favorite cookie. They are studded with pepitas—hulled pumpkin seeds—sesame seeds and sunflower seeds. But don't stop there . . . feel free to substitute hemp seeds or flax seeds for a whole new taste. Snacking on nuts and seeds satisfies hunger and also helps control appetite during a meal that follows in the next two hours. Participants in a study who snacked on rice cakes actually overate at mealtime, while subjects eating nuts ate less fat and fewer calories at meals.

¾ cup whole wheat pastry flour

½ teaspoon ground cinnamon

½ teaspoon baking soda

½ teaspoon salt

1½ cups old-fashioned rolled oats

¾ cup sunflower seeds (if using salted seeds, omit the ½ teaspoon salt)

¼ cup sesame seeds

⅓ cup pepitas or hulled pumpkin seeds

½ cup olive oil

¾ cup brown sugar, packed

1 egg

1 teaspoon vanilla extract

Preheat oven to 350°F and line a baking sheet with parchment paper.

In a large bowl, combine the flour, cinnamon, baking soda, salt, oats, sunflower seeds, sesame seeds, and pepitas. Make a well in the center.

In a medium bowl, whisk together the olive oil, brown sugar, egg, and vanilla extract.

Pour the wet ingredients into the dry and stir to combine.

Drop the cookies by rounded spoonfuls onto the prepared pan.

Bake for 11–12 minutes or until lightly browned at the edges. Bake the cookies one pan at a time.

Allow to cool on the baking sheet for 2 minutes and then transfer to a wire rack to complete cooling.

Makes 4 dozen cookies.

DAIRY-FREE

Hazelnut Lemon Biscotti

The name biscotti comes from the roots "bis" and "cotto"—literally meaning "twice" and "baked." When Italians in the region of Tuscany first created biscotti centuries ago, they were careful to bake the cookies twice, allowing them to take their unique shape and develop their signature crisp texture. This recipe would make the Tuscans proud!

1	cup hazelnuts, toasted and skinned	1¼	cups sugar
2¾	cups all-purpose flour	¼	cup olive oil
1	cup whole wheat pastry flour	2	tablespoons lemon zest, about 3 lemons
1	teaspoon baking powder	1	tablespoon vanilla extract
1	teaspoon salt	2	tablespoons lemon juice
3	large eggs	⅓	cup milk

To toast and skin hazelnuts: Place hazelnuts in a single layer on a baking pan in a preheated 300°F oven for 25–30 minutes, or until the skins are lightly colored and the skins are cracked. Wrap the nuts in a clean kitchen towel and let them sit for 5 minutes. Rub the nuts to remove the skins.

Preheat oven to 350°F. Line two baking sheets with parchment paper.

In a large bowl, combine the flours, baking powder, and salt.

In another large bowl, whisk the eggs until they are foamy. Gradually whisk in the sugar and continue whisking until the mixture is pale yellow and light, about 4 minutes. Whisk in the olive oil. Add the lemon zest, vanilla extract, lemon juice, and milk; mix well.

Add the wet ingredients to the dry and stir to combine thoroughly. Then mix in the hazelnuts.

Turn out the dough onto a lightly floured work surface and divide in half. Shape each half into a 10 x 4-inch rectangular log. Place the logs about 2 inches apart on one of the prepared baking sheets.

Bake the logs in the center of the oven until they are puffed and golden, 25–30 minutes. Remove from the oven and let cool on a wire rack for 10 minutes. Leave the oven on.

Place the logs on a clean cutting surface. With a serrated knife, create the biscotti by cutting at a slight diagonal across the logs, making ½- to ¾-inch slices (15–20 pieces). Lay cookies cut-side down on the parchment-lined cookie sheets and bake for 15 minutes. Remove the cookies from the oven, turn over, and bake for an additional 10 minutes on the other side.

Transfer the biscotti to a wire rack and cool completely. Store in an airtight container for up to 3 weeks.

Makes 3–4 dozen biscotti.

Hazelnut Sables

People who like the distinctive flavor of hazelnuts will love these delicately flavored gems. They are wonderful served with tea. The unbaked dough can be frozen, in log form, for up to 1 month— thaw, slice, and bake cookies as needed for special company.

⅔	cup hazelnuts, toasted and skins removed	I	whole egg
I	cup whole wheat pastry flour	I	egg yolk
½	cup all-purpose flour	⅔	cup plus 2 tablespoons confectioners' sugar
½	teaspoon cinnamon		
¼	teaspoon baking soda	⅓	cup olive oil
½	teaspoon salt	I	teaspoon vanilla extract

To toast and skin hazelnuts: Place hazelnuts in a single layer on a baking pan in a preheated 300°F oven for 25–30 minutes, or until the skins are lightly colored and the skins are cracked. Wrap the nuts in a clean kitchen towel and let them sit for 5 minutes. Rub the nuts to remove the skins.

In a small bowl, combine the flours, cinnamon, baking soda, and salt.

Using a food processor, finely grind the toasted hazelnuts and 2 tablespoons of confectioners' sugar.

In a medium bowl, beat the whole egg, egg yolk, and ⅔ cup confectioners' sugar with a handheld mixer until light in color and very thick, about 5 minutes. With the beater running, slowly add the olive oil in a steady stream. Add the vanilla extract and beat to combine. Stir in the nuts.

Stir dry ingredients into wet until well combined.

Turn the dough out onto a lightly floured board and divide in half. Shape each piece into a 7- or 8-inch log and wrap tightly in waxed paper or parchment paper. Refrigerate a minimum of 4 hours and up to 2 days. (You can freeze the dough at this point. Freeze the tightly wrapped, unbaked logs for up to 1 month. Prior to baking, thaw in the refrigerator.)

Preheat oven to 350°F.

When ready to bake, remove from refrigerator and unwrap. Slice log into ¼-inch slices and bake for 14–16 minutes or until the bottoms are slightly brown. Cool on a wire rack.

Makes 6 dozen cookies.

DAIRY FREE

Hazelnut Sables

Lemon Sugar Cookies

These sugar cookies have a crispy, sparkly exterior and a robust lemon flavor. Great on a summer day or with a cup of steamy green tea.

1 cup all-purpose flour	½ cup plus 1 tablespoon olive oil
1 cup whole wheat pastry flour	1 tablespoon lemon zest, from 1 large
1 cup plus 2 tablespoons granulated sugar	lemon
½ teaspoon baking soda	1 teaspoon vanilla extract
¼ teaspoon salt	2 tablespoons lemon juice

In a small bowl, combine flours, 1 cup sugar, baking soda, and salt. In another small bowl, blend olive oil, lemon zest, vanilla extract, and lemon juice.

Add the liquid ingredients to the dry, and using a large spoon, stir in dry ingredients until uniform. Cover and chill dough for 2 hours or overnight.

Preheat oven to 350°F and line baking sheet with parchment paper.

Roll dough into balls 1 inch in diameter. Roll in remaining granulated sugar and place on parchment-lined baking sheet.

Bake for 12–15 minutes. Cookies will look puffed and be soft to the touch. Cool on sheet for 2 minutes, then transfer to a wire rack to cool completely.

Store in an airtight container.

Makes 4 dozen cookies.

DAIRY-FREE

Maple Cinnamon Graham Crackers

These graham crackers are slightly sweet and full of mellow maple flavor. This dough is easy enough to handle, so get kids to help. Cut into playful shapes or use cookie cutters for some added flair. If you are so inclined, sprinkle the tops with plain or cinnamon sugar.

1½	cups whole wheat pastry flour	⅓	cup pure maple syrup
1½	cups all-purpose flour	½	teaspoon vanilla extract
1	teaspoon baking powder	¼	cup olive oil
½	teaspoon salt		*Cinnamon sugar:*
¼	teaspoon cinnamon	2	tablespoons granulated sugar
1	egg	½	teaspoon cinnamon

Preheat oven to 375°F and line two baking sheets with parchment paper.

In a large bowl, combine the flours, baking powder, salt, and ¼ teaspoon cinnamon and stir to mix. Make a well in the center.

In a separate bowl, lightly whisk the egg, then add the maple syrup, vanilla extract, and olive oil. Whisk to combine these ingredients.

Pour the wet ingredients into the well in the center of the dry ingredients and stir to combine. Using your hands, massage the dough to bring it together into a ball.

Use a surface such as a pastry board or countertop for rolling the dough. Divide the dough into 2 balls and place between 2 layers of waxed paper. Roll the dough to a thickness of ⅛ inch.

Cut dough into a variety of shapes—squares, triangles, or circles (with a biscuit or cookie cutter). Pierce the crackers several times with a fork.

Transfer to the prepared baking sheet and bake for 15 minutes. The crackers will be firm to the touch. Do not let them brown.

Transfer to a wire rack to cool completely. Store in an airtight container.

Makes about 2½ dozen crackers.

DAIRY-FREE

Maple Coconut Cookies

Living in rural New England has its advantages, including access to locally produced maple syrup. This recipe brings to mind the early signs of spring—sap buckets hanging on the sugar maples and steam rising from the sugar shacks.

1¼	cups all-purpose flour	¾	cup maple syrup
¾	cup whole wheat pastry flour	¼	cup water
1	tablespoon baking powder	¼	cup olive oil
¼	teaspoon salt	1	teaspoon vanilla extract
¼	teaspoon cinnamon	½	teaspoon maple extract
1¼	cups sweetened flaked coconut		

Preheat oven to 350°F and line two baking sheets with parchment paper.

In a small bowl, combine the flours, baking powder, salt, and cinnamon. Stir in the coconut, breaking up any lumps with your fingers.

In another bowl, mix the maple syrup, water, olive oil, and vanilla and maple extracts. Stir the dry ingredients into the wet, just until mixed.

Drop onto the prepared sheets by rounded teaspoonfuls.

Bake for 12–14 minutes or until firm to the touch and slightly browned. Allow cookies to cool 2 minutes on pans, then transfer to wire racks to cool completely.

Makes 3 dozen cookies.

DAIRY-FREE

Mincemeat Oatmeal Cookies

Mincemeat is an old-fashioned mixture of nuts, raisins, dried fruits such as apples and pears, citrus peel, spices, beef, and sometimes brandy or rum. The amount of saturated fat in mincemeat is very small, and it contributes a rich flavor to these chewy, flavorful oatmeal cookies. Vegetarian forms of mincemeat are sometimes available.

3	cups quick-cooking oats		½	cup olive oil
I	cup all-purpose flour		I	teaspoon vanilla extract
½	cup whole wheat pastry flour		3	tablespoons water (or I tablespoon water
I	teaspoon baking soda			and 2 tablespoons spiced rum, such as
½	teaspoon salt			Captain Morgan's)
3	eggs		I	(9-ounce) package of condensed mince-
I⅓	cups brown sugar, packed			meat, crumbled

Preheat oven to 350°F and line two baking sheets with parchment paper.

In a large bowl, combine the oats, flours, baking soda, and salt. Set aside.

In another bowl, whisk together the eggs, brown sugar, olive oil, vanilla extract, and water.

Add the wet mixture to the dry and stir to combine. Mix in the crumbled mincemeat. (The mincemeat comes in a solid block. To crumble, slice into pieces first.)

Drop by rounded spoonfuls onto the prepared baking sheets and bake for 10–12 minutes or until the cookies are lightly browned.

Allow the cookies to cool on the pans for 5 minutes, then transfer to a wire rack to cool completely.

Makes 5 dozen cookies.

DAIRY-FREE

Natural Peanut Butter Cookies

So many recipes use processed peanut butter that has added fats, sugar, and preservatives. This recipe uses natural peanut butter, which allows the true flavor of the nuts to shine through. The preparation is slightly updated, but there are also directions for the classic fork hatch design.

1	cup all-purpose flour	2	teaspoons vanilla extract
½	cup whole wheat pastry flour	¼	cup olive oil
½	teaspoon baking soda	1	cup natural peanut butter, creamy or
½	teaspoon salt		chunky
2	eggs	½	cup finely ground peanuts for rolling the
1	cup brown sugar		cookies
¾	cup granulated sugar		

Preheat oven to 350°F.

In a small bowl, combine the flours, baking soda, and salt.

In another bowl, whisk together the eggs, sugars, and vanilla extract. Stir in the olive oil and peanut butter.

Add the dry ingredients and stir until combined.

Shape the cookies into 1–1½-inch diameter balls. Roll in the prepared ground nuts. (If you prefer the classic fork design to the cookies, flatten the balls first with the tines of a fork dipped in milk.)

Bake for 13–15 minutes.

Transfer to a wire rack to cool.

Makes 3 dozen cookies.

DAIRY-FREE

Oat Bran Crisps (a.k.a. "Lunch Box Louies")

My husband's Great Aunt Betty would have loved these cookies. They are chock-full of whole grains yet have a light crisp texture. To me, these are the ideal lunch box cookie. My kids think so, too!

1½ cups old-fashioned rolled oats, not quick-cooking	¾ cup brown sugar
	¾ cup granulated sugar
1½ cups oat bran	¾ cup olive oil
1 cup whole wheat pastry flour	2 eggs
1 teaspoon baking soda	2 teaspoons vanilla extract
1 teaspoon salt	1 cup raisins or chocolate chips
1½ teaspoons cinnamon	½ cup chopped walnuts

Preheat oven to 350°F and line two baking sheets with parchment paper.

In a small bowl, combine oats, oat bran, flour, baking soda, salt, and cinnamon.

Using a handheld mixer beat the sugars and olive oil in a large bowl. Add the eggs, one at a time, beating well after each addition. Add the vanilla extract and beat to combine.

Using a large spoon stir in the dry ingredients. Add the raisins or chocolate chips and the nuts and stir to distribute.

Drop by rounded tablespoonfuls onto the prepared baking sheets. Since these cookies tend to spread, space them at least 4 inches apart on pans.

Bake for 12–14 minutes. Cool 5 minutes on the sheets, then remove to wire rack.

Store in an airtight container.

Makes 5 dozen cookies.

DAIRY FREE

Oatmeal Drop Cookies

Always a favorite, these oatmeal cookies are loaded with juicy raisins and a hint of cinnamon.

½	cup whole wheat pastry flour	I	tablespoon molasses
½	cup all-purpose flour	½	cup olive oil
½	teaspoon baking powder	I	egg, beaten
¼	teaspoon baking soda	2	tablespoons water
½	teaspoon salt	I	teaspoon vanilla extract
I	teaspoon ground cinnamon	½	cup raisins
½	teaspoon ground ginger	½	cup chopped walnuts (optional)
¾	cup light brown sugar, packed	½	cup chocolate chips (optional)
I½	cups old-fashioned rolled oats		

Preheat oven to 350°F.

In a medium bowl, combine flours, baking powder, baking soda, salt, cinnamon, and ginger. Stir in the brown sugar and oats.

Make a well in the center of the dry ingredients and add molasses, olive oil, egg, water, and vanilla extract. Stir vigorously until dry ingredients are moistened. Stir in raisins, walnuts, and/or chocolate chips.

Drop by rounded tablespoonfuls 2 inches apart onto an ungreased cookie sheet.

Bake for 13–15 minutes or until done, rotating cookie sheets halfway through baking time. Remove cookies immediately onto a wire rack to cool.

Makes 2½–3 dozen cookies.

DAIRY-FREE

Pineapple Macadamia Nut Cookies

Macadamias—one of the world's finest nuts—are characterized by their crisp texture, delicate flavor, versatility of use, and long shelf life. They are a source of healthy fats and are rich in antioxidants.

1¼ cups all-purpose flour	¾ cup granulated sugar
1 teaspoon baking soda	¼ cup brown sugar
½ teaspoon salt	1 tablespoon dark or Captain Morgan's
⅛ teaspoon freshly ground nutmeg	spiced rum (or water)
⅓ cup olive oil	¾ cup finely chopped dried sweetened
1 teaspoon vanilla extract	pineapple
½ teaspoon almond extract	¾ cup chopped Macadamia nuts
1 egg	

Preheat oven to 350°F and line a baking sheet with parchment paper.

In a small bowl, combine the flour, baking soda, salt, and nutmeg.

In a large bowl, whisk together the olive oil, vanilla and almond extracts, egg, sugars, and rum (or water). Add the dry ingredients to the wet and stir until well combined, then add the chopped pineapple and macadamia nuts.

Drop by rounded spoonfuls onto the prepared baking sheet.

Bake one pan of cookies at a time.

Bake for 12–14 minutes or until slightly brown at the edges. Allow to cool on the sheets for 5 minutes, then transfer to a wire rack to cool completely.

Makes 3 dozen cookies.

DAIRY FREE

Pumpkin Butterscotch Cake Cookies

I am very partial to pumpkin—I love the color, moistness, and flavor it adds to baked goods. These cookies are one of my favorites. There is something about the combination of butterscotch, walnuts, and pumpkin that is magical to say the least!

1	cup all-purpose flour	2	eggs
1	cup whole wheat pastry flour	1	cup granulated sugar
1½	teaspoons baking powder	½	cup olive oil
1	teaspoon baking soda	1	cup canned pumpkin
½	teaspoon salt	1	teaspoon vanilla extract
1½	teaspoons cinnamon	½	cup butterscotch chips
1	teaspoon ginger	½	cup chopped walnuts

Preheat oven to 325°F and line two baking sheets with parchment paper.

In a small bowl, combine the flours, baking powder, baking soda, salt, cinnamon, and ginger.

In a large bowl, whisk together the eggs, sugar, and olive oil until smooth. Add the pumpkin and vanilla extract and whisk until incorporated.

Stir the dry ingredients into the wet with a few broad strokes. Add the butterscotch chips and walnuts and continue stirring gently until well combined.

Drop by tablespoonfuls onto the prepared baking sheets.

Bake for 14–16 minutes or until the cookies feel firm to the touch. Cool cookies on the pans for 2 minutes, then transfer to wire racks to cool completely.

Makes 3 dozen cookies.

DAIRY-FREE

Pumpkin Cookies

These cookies are soft and slightly cake-like. My daughters love these with a glass of cold milk and some apple slices for an after-school snack.

I	cup all-purpose flour	¼	teaspoon ground cloves
I	cup whole wheat pastry flour	I	egg
2	tablespoons wheat germ	I	teaspoon vanilla extract
I	teaspoon baking soda	½	cup olive oil
I	teaspoon baking powder	I	cup canned pumpkin
½	teaspoon salt	I	cup brown sugar, packed
I	teaspoon cinnamon	I	cup currants or raisins
½	teaspoon ginger	½	cup chopped walnuts

Preheat oven to 350°F and line two baking sheets with parchment paper.

In a small bowl, combine the flours, wheat germ, baking soda, baking powder, salt, cinnamon, ginger, and cloves.

In another bowl, blend the egg, vanilla, olive oil, pumpkin, and brown sugar with a whisk. Add the dry ingredients and stir until combined. Stir in the raisins and walnuts.

Drop by rounded spoonfuls onto the prepared baking sheets.

Bake for 12–15 minutes or until just the top is firm to the touch.

Transfer to a wire rack to cool completely.

Makes 3½ dozen cookies.

DAIRY FREE

Super Fruit and Nut Cookies

These cookies are a great mid-morning snack. With figs, currants, cranberries, and almonds, they are a hearty taste explosion!

1	cup all-purpose flour		¼	cup olive oil
½	cup whole wheat pastry flour		1	teaspoon vanilla extract
½	cup oat bran		2	eggs
½	teaspoon baking soda		¼	cup finely chopped dried figs
¼	teaspoon salt		¼	cup currants
½	teaspoon cinnamon		¼	cup dried cranberries
¼	teaspoon allspice		¼	cup sliced almonds plus 2 tablespoons for
¾	cup brown sugar			tops of cookies

Preheat oven to 350°F and line two baking sheets with parchment paper.

In a small bowl, combine the flours, oat bran, baking soda, salt, cinnamon, and allspice. Set aside.

In a large bowl, combine the brown sugar, olive oil, vanilla, and eggs and whisk to blend. Stir in figs, currants, and cranberries.

Add dry ingredients to the wet and stir to combine. Stir in the ¼ cup sliced almonds.

Drop the cookies by rounded spoonfuls onto the prepared baking sheets. Sprinkle a few sliced almonds on the top of each cookie.

Bake for 12–14 minutes or until lightly browned.

Cool for 2 minutes on the sheets, then transfer to a wire rack to cool completely.

Makes 2 dozen cookies.

DAIRY-FREE

True Spice Cookies

Both mace and nutmeg are derived from the fruit of the same tree, Myristica fragrans. Mace is the thin, bright red, lace-like covering over the shell of the nutmeg. Its flavor is similar to nutmeg but more delicate. So if you don't have the mace on-hand, substitute ¾ teaspoon nutmeg for the 1 teaspoon of mace.

¾	cup olive oil	1½	teaspoons baking soda
¼	cup molasses	½	teaspoon salt
1	cup granulated sugar	1½	tablespoons ground cinnamon
2	eggs	1½	tablespoons ground ginger
1	teaspoon vanilla extract	1	teaspoon mace
1¾	cups all-purpose flour	2	teaspoons ground cloves
1	cup whole wheat pastry flour	¼	cup granulated sugar

In a large bowl, whisk together olive oil, molasses, granulated sugar, eggs, and vanilla extract.

In a separate bowl, combine flours, baking soda, salt, cinnamon, ginger, mace, and cloves.

Add the dry ingredients to the wet and stir until well combined. Cover the dough and refrigerate overnight.

Preheat oven to 350°F and line two baking sheets with parchment paper. Place remaining ¼ cup granulated sugar in a small bowl.

Form the dough into 1½-inch balls and roll in granulated sugar. Place on baking sheets and bake for 10–12 minutes or until tops crack.

Allow cookies to cool for 5 minutes on baking sheets and then transfer to a wire rack to cool completely.

Makes roughly 3 dozen cookies.

DAIRY-FREE

Vanilla Sugar Cookies

This healthy classic is a hit with children and adults alike. Serve them with fresh fruit on a summer evening or with hot cocoa after a day spent sledding—either way they are sure to disappear!

3	eggs	1	cup whole wheat pastry flour
1½	cups granulated sugar	2½	cups all-purpose flour
½	cup olive oil	2	teaspoons baking powder
1	tablespoon vanilla extract	¼	teaspoon salt
⅓	cup natural applesauce		

Using a handheld mixer, beat eggs, sugar, and olive oil until light and slightly thickened. Add vanilla extract and applesauce and beat to incorporate.

Place flours, baking powder, and salt in a separate bowl and mix slightly. Using a spoon, stir the dry mixture into the egg mixture.

Chill the dough for 4 hours or longer.

Preheat the oven to 350°F.

Working with a teaspoon of dough at a time, shape into a ball using your hands. Roll each ball in granulated sugar and then place on a cookie sheet. With the flat bottom of a drinking glass, flatten the cookies to the thickness of ½ inch.

Bake for 12–14 minutes. Remove from sheets and cool on a wire rack.

Makes 3½ dozen 2-inch cookies.

DAIRY FREE

CHAPTER 8
MUFFINS

Almond Poppy Seed Muffins

The aroma of these muffins baking fills the house with unmistakable warmth and energy—enough to entice even the latest of sleepers from their beds!

1	cup all-purpose flour	¾	cup low-fat milk
½	cup whole wheat pastry flour	2	large eggs
1	cup granulated sugar	1	teaspoon vanilla extract
1	teaspoon baking powder	1½	teaspoons almond extract
½	teaspoon salt	2	tablespoons poppy seeds
½	cup olive oil	½	cup sliced almonds, divided

Preheat oven to 375°F. Using paper liners, line 12 muffin cups.

In a small bowl combine flours, sugar, baking powder, and salt. Set aside.

In another bowl, whisk together olive oil, milk, eggs, vanilla extract, and almond extract until smooth. Stir in poppy seeds. Add dry ingredients and all but 2 tablespoons of the sliced almonds. Stir just until moistened.

Fill prepared muffin cups about three-fourths full and sprinkle with reserved sliced almonds.

Bake for 18–22 minutes or until a toothpick inserted into the center of a muffin comes out clean.

Cool on a wire rack. Serve warm.

Store in an airtight container or freeze for up to 1 month.

Makes 12 muffins.

Apple Butter Muffins

Be sure to include your children in kitchen duties—they are great at putting paper liners in a muffin pan or stirring. Both of my daughters learned fractions at my elbow in the kitchen. Cooking is an excellent way to teach math and science!

1	cup all-purpose flour	¼	teaspoon ginger
¾	cup whole wheat pastry flour	¼	teaspoon salt
⅓	cup granulated sugar	1	egg
2	teaspoons baking powder	¾	cup milk
½	teaspoon cinnamon	¼	cup olive oil
¼	teaspoon nutmeg	½	cup apple butter
¼	teaspoon allspice	¼	cup finely chopped walnuts

Preheat oven to 400°F and line 12 muffin cups with paper liners.

In a medium bowl, combine the flours, sugar, baking powder, cinnamon, nutmeg, allspice, ginger, and salt. Make a well in the center.

In another bowl, whisk together the egg, milk, olive oil, and apple butter.

Pour the wet ingredients into the dry and stir until nearly combined, then add the walnuts and continue stirring until combined. Do not overmix.

Divide the batter among the prepared muffin cups.

Bake for 15–18 minutes or until a toothpick inserted into the center of a muffin comes out clean.

Transfer to a wire rack to cool.

Makes 12 muffins.

Apple Harvest Muffins

These scrumptious muffins are great for breakfast, snacking, or brunch.

I	cup all-purpose flour	2	eggs
½	cup whole wheat pastry flour	I	cup low-fat or fat-free sour cream
½	cup granulated sugar	¼	cup olive oil
2	teaspoons baking powder	I	teaspoon vanilla extract
I	teaspoon cinnamon	I	cup finely diced, peeled apples, such as
¼	teaspoon allspice		Granny Smith or other tart apple
¼	teaspoon baking soda	½	cup finely chopped walnuts
¼	teaspoon salt		

Preheat oven to 375°F. Line 12 muffin cups with foil cups or spray with cooking spray.

In a large bowl, combine flours, sugar, baking powder, cinnamon, allspice, baking soda, and salt. Make a well in the center of the dry ingredients.

In a separate bowl, whisk together eggs, sour cream, olive oil, and vanilla extract. Add the wet ingredients to the dry and stir just until moist. Gently fold in apple and walnuts.

Divide batter into prepared muffin cups.

Bake for 20–25 minutes or until a toothpick inserted into the center a muffin comes out clean. Let cool in the pan for 5 minutes. Remove from pan and cool completely on a wire rack.

Store in an airtight container for up to 5 days or freeze up to 1 month.

Makes 12 muffins.

Butterscotch Apple Muffins

These are one of my daughter's favorite muffins—they are delicious warm. If you are a pistachio fan, use pistachio pudding, ½ cup chopped pistachio nuts, and ½ cup well-drained crushed pineapple in place of the butterscotch pudding and grated apple. Great for St. Patty's Day!

1	cup all-purpose flour	1	egg
¾	cup whole wheat pastry flour	¼	cup granulated sugar
1	tablespoon baking powder	1¼	cups milk
¼	teaspoon salt	½	cup apple, peeled and grated
1	(3-ounce) package instant butterscotch pudding	1	teaspoon vanilla extract
		½	cup butterscotch chips
¼	cup olive oil		

Preheat oven to 400°F and line 12 muffin cups with paper liners.

In a medium bowl, combine flours, baking powder, salt, and pudding mix.

In a large bowl, whisk together olive oil, egg, sugar, milk, apple, and vanilla extract.

Add the flour mixture and stir just until blended and fold in the butterscotch chips. The batter will be very thick.

Divide batter among the prepared muffin cups and bake for 22–26 minutes.

Transfer muffins to a wire rack to cool.

Makes 12 muffins.

Chocolate Banana Dream Muffins

Banana makes these fun little muffins moist and very aromatic. If you are a real chocolate lover, save a few of the mini chips to sprinkle on the tops of the muffins. Mini muffins are great when you just want a little taste—use them for snacking with a plate of fruit or for your next tea party!

⅔	cup mashed ripe bananas		¾	cup all-purpose flour
½	cup low-fat or fat-free milk		I	cup old-fashioned or quick-cooking oats
½	cup light brown sugar, packed		⅓	cup unsweetened cocoa powder, sifted
⅓	cup olive oil		I	tablespoon baking powder
I	egg		¼	teaspoon baking soda
I	teaspoon vanilla extract		¼	teaspoon salt
½	cup whole wheat pastry flour		½	cup semisweet mini chocolate chips

Preheat oven to 375°F. Line 36 mini muffin cups with paper liners.

In a small bowl, whisk together banana, milk, brown sugar, olive oil, egg, and vanilla.

Combine flours, oats, cocoa powder, baking powder, baking soda, and salt. Add the wet ingredients to the dry and stir just until moistened. Gently fold in chocolate chips.

Fill muffin cups three-fourths full.

Bake for 14–16 minutes or until a wooden toothpick inserted into the center of a muffin comes out clean.

Cool for 5 minutes in the pans, then remove to a wire rack and cool completely. Serve warm or at room temperature. Store in an airtight container up to 5 days or freeze up to 1 month.

Makes 3 dozen mini muffins.

Cranberry Orange Muffins

Bake these scrumptious muffins the night before and store in an airtight container to enjoy first thing in the morning.

1 cup all-purpose flour	¾ cup orange juice (about 1 large orange)
1 cup whole wheat pastry flour	¼ cup olive oil
1 cup sugar	1 large egg
1½ teaspoons baking powder	1½ cups chopped cranberries
1 teaspoon salt	½ teaspoon cinnamon
½ teaspoon baking soda	1 tablespoon turbinado (coarse) sugar
1 tablespoon grated orange rind (about one large orange)	

Preheat oven to 400°F. Line 12 muffin cups with paper liners.

In a large bowl, combine flours, sugar, baking powder, salt, and baking soda.

In another bowl, whisk orange rind, juice, olive oil, and egg to combine. Add the dry ingredients to the wet and stir just until moist. Fold in cranberries.

Spoon the batter into prepared muffin pans. Sprinkle lightly with cinnamon and sugar.

Bake for 15–18 minutes or until the muffins spring back when touched lightly in the center.

Run a knife around the edges of the muffins and carefully remove from the pan. Cool on a wire rack.

Makes 12 large muffins.

DAIRY-FREE

Lemon Ginger Muffins

Loaded with fresh ginger root and lemon zest, these muffins aren't just for breakfast!

1	lemon	½	cup olive oil
1	cup granulated sugar, divided	1	cup low-fat or fat-free buttermilk
⅔	cup fresh ginger root, peeled and finely chopped	1	cup whole wheat pastry flour
		1¾	cups all-purpose flour
2	large eggs	½	teaspoon salt
1	teaspoon vanilla extract	1	teaspoon baking soda

Preheat the oven to 350°F. Line 18 muffin cups with paper liners.

With a paring knife, vegetable peeler, or zester, remove the yellow peel from the lemon. Avoid the bitter white pith of the lemon peel. Place ½ cup of granulated sugar, fresh ginger, and lemon zest in the food processor. Scrape down sides as needed. Process this mixture until finely puréed.

Transfer the ginger mixture to a bowl. Whisk in eggs, vanilla, olive oil, and buttermilk.

Combine the remaining ½ cup sugar, flours, salt, and baking soda in a bowl. Stir the wet mixture into the dry just until blended.

Divide the batter among the prepared muffin cups. Bake for 25 minutes or until toothpick inserted in the center of a muffin comes out clean.

Makes 18 muffins.

Morning Glory Muffins

These muffins are truly like a meal. They are packed with fruit and nuts. Pair with a cup of yogurt for the perfect breakfast on the run.

1	cup all-purpose flour	1	cup olive oil
1	cup whole wheat pastry flour	1¼	cups granulated sugar
2	teaspoons baking soda	2	teaspoons vanilla extract
2	teaspoons cinnamon	1	cup peeled, finely grated carrots
¼	teaspoon cloves	1	Granny Smith apple, peeled and grated
¼	teaspoon nutmeg	½	cup raisins or currants
½	teaspoon salt	½	cup shredded, sweetened coconut
3	eggs, lightly beaten	½	cup walnuts or pecans

Preheat oven to 350°F and line 24 muffin cups with paper liners.

In a small bowl, combine flours, baking soda, cinnamon, cloves, nutmeg, and salt; mix well.

In a large bowl, whisk together eggs, olive oil, sugar, vanilla, carrots, apple, raisins, coconut, and nuts.

Add the dry ingredients and stir just until moistened.

Fill muffin cups three-fourths full and bake for 15–20 minutes or until a toothpick inserted into the center of a muffin comes out clean.

Cool in the pans for 5 minutes, then transfer to a cooling rack. Serve warm. Store leftovers in an airtight container or freeze for up to 1 month.

Makes 24 muffins.

DAIRY FREE

Pineapple Coconut Muffins

Pineapple is a great source of manganese, which is important for bone health and building connective tissue in your body. Plus, it tastes great and makes these tropical muffins moist and fragrant.

Topping:

⅓ cup light brown sugar, packed
¼ cup all-purpose flour
½ cup shredded coconut
2 tablespoons old-fashioned rolled oats
2 tablespoons olive oil

1⅓ cups all-purpose flour
⅔ cup old-fashioned rolled oats
1 teaspoon baking powder

½ teaspoon baking soda
¼ teaspoon salt
1 egg
⅓ cup brown sugar, packed
½ cup granulated sugar
⅓ cup olive oil
1 teaspoon vanilla extract
1 can crushed pineapple, well drained
1 cup low-fat or fat-free buttermilk
⅓ cup shredded, sweetened coconut

Preheat oven to 400°F. Lightly oil 18 muffin cups or line with paper liners.

In a large bowl, combine all the topping ingredients: ⅓ cup brown sugar, flour, coconut, 2 tablespoons oats, and olive oil, and rub together with fingers until crumbs form. Set aside.

In a large bowl, combine flour, oats, baking powder, baking soda, and salt. Make a well in the center of the mixture.

In another bowl, whisk together egg, brown and granulated sugars, olive oil, vanilla, pineapple, and buttermilk.

Add the liquid ingredients to the dry and stir just until moist. Gently fold in coconut. Do not overmix.

Divide the batter among the prepared muffin cups. Sprinkle with prepared topping.

Bake for 20–24 minutes or until a toothpick inserted into the center of a muffin comes out clean.

Cool in the pan for 5 minutes, then transfer to a wire rack to cool completely.

Makes 18 muffins.

Pumpkin Muffins

Pumpkin is a great source of vitamin A in the form of beta-carotene. Research has shown that beta-carotene-rich foods help lower the incidence of some cancers. Vitamin A also plays a role in good vision, healthy skin, a strong immune system, and bone and teeth development. Pumpkin is also a good source of vitamin C, which helps fight infection. So enjoy!

1	cup all-purpose flour	½	teaspoon ginger
½	cup whole wheat pastry flour	¼	teaspoon ground cloves
½	cup granulated sugar	¼	cup olive oil
½	cup brown sugar	½	cup low-fat or fat-free buttermilk
½	teaspoon baking powder	1	cup canned pumpkin
1	teaspoon baking soda	¼	cup unsweetened applesauce
½	teaspoon salt	2	large eggs
1	teaspoon cinnamon		

Preheat oven to 375°F. Coat a 1-cup muffin pan lightly with cooking spray.

In a large bowl, combine flours, sugars, baking powder, baking soda, salt, cinnamon, ginger, and cloves. Mix to combine.

In another bowl, whisk together the olive oil, buttermilk, pumpkin, applesauce, and eggs to combine. Add to the dry ingredients and stir just until moist.

Spoon the batter into prepared muffin pans.

Bake for 20 minutes or until the muffins spring back when touched lightly in the center.

Cool on a wire rack.

Makes 12 large muffins.

Super Bran Muffins

Healthy, absolutely delicious, and good for you—what more can you ask of a muffin? Top these hearty muffins with honey or jam for a real treat first thing in the morning!

1	cup all-purpose flour	⅓	cup golden brown sugar, packed
½	cup whole wheat flour	¼	cup olive oil
½	cup oat bran	2	large eggs
1	teaspoon ground cinnamon	1¼	cups low-fat or fat-free buttermilk
½	teaspoon ground nutmeg	1	teaspoon grated lemon zest
2	teaspoons baking powder	2	teaspoons vanilla extract
1	teaspoon baking soda	½	cup raisins or currants (optional)
½	teaspoon salt		

Preheat oven to 400°F. Line 12 muffin cups with foil liners.

In a medium bowl, combine flours, oat bran, cinnamon, nutmeg, baking powder, baking soda, and salt.

In a large bowl, whisk the brown sugar and olive oil, then add eggs, buttermilk, lemon zest, and vanilla extract. Whisk until well blended. Stir in raisins, if using.

Stir in dry ingredients, mixing just until moistened. Divide batter among muffin cups.

Bake muffins until browned on top and tester inserted into center comes out clean, about 18–20 minutes.

Cool on rack. Serve warm.

Store any leftover muffins in an airtight container or freeze for up to 1 month.

Makes 12 muffins.

Super Cinnamon Blueberry Muffins

Turbinado sugar (like Sugar in the Raw™), used to top these delicious muffins, is a form of unrefined cane sugar that gets its name from the process of spinning the crystals from raw cane sugar. Other types of unrefined sugars include jaggery (from India), demerara (from Mauritius), and muscovado (from Barbados). These coarse, naturally colored sugars are not to be confused with "brown sugar," which is formed by adding molasses back to refined, white sugar. There is evidence that jaggery, high in minerals and fiber, protects against lung damage in Indian miners.

⅓ cup olive oil
½ cup light brown sugar, packed
½ cup granulated sugar
½ cup whole or 2 percent milk
1 large egg
1 cup all-purpose flour
½ cup whole wheat pastry flour

1½ teaspoons baking powder
1 teaspoon cinnamon
½ teaspoon salt
1½ cups fresh blueberries (or if frozen, partially thawed)
Turbinado sugar (or other coarse "raw" sugar) for muffins tops

Line a muffin pan with 12 paper cups. Adjust rack to the upper third of the oven, and preheat to 375°F.

Whisk together olive oil, sugars, milk, and egg in a bowl until combined well. In another large bowl, whisk together flours, baking powder, cinnamon, and salt. Add milk mixture and stir until just combined. Fold in blueberries gently.

Divide batter among prepared muffin cups and sprinkle with coarse/turbinado sugar.

Bake for about 25–30 minutes or until golden brown and a toothpick inserted into center of a muffin comes out clean.

Let cool in muffin pans for 5 minutes, then remove and cool completely on a wire rack.

Store muffins in an airtight container or freeze up to 1 month.

Makes 12 muffins.

CHAPTER 9
COFFEECAKES

Best-Ever Cinnamon Rolls

Consider making these rolls ahead, without the glaze. Then on that special morning, heat and glaze with ease. You will enjoying your morning and a wonderful breakfast in no time.

⅓	cup warm water (110°F)		1	cup whole wheat pastry flour
2¼	teaspoons dry active yeast or one package yeast		*Filling:*	
1	tablespoon granulated sugar		½	cup light brown sugar, packed
¼	cup olive oil		½	cup chopped walnuts or pecans
¼	cup granulated sugar		2	tablespoons olive oil
½	low-fat or fat-free sour cream		1½	teaspoons cinnamon
1	egg		*Glaze (optional):*	
1	teaspoon vanilla extract		¾	cup sifted powdered or confectioners' sugar
½	teaspoon salt		2–3	tablespoons orange juice
2¼	cups all-purpose flour, divided		¼	teaspoon vanilla extract

In a small bowl, combine the water, yeast, and 1 tablespoon granulated sugar. Let stand 10 minutes or until foamy.

In a large bowl, combine olive oil, egg, vanilla, and ¼ cup granulated sugar using handheld mixer. Add 1 cup of all-purpose flour and beat until well combined. Add yeast mixture and whole wheat pastry flour and beat until well blended, about 2 minutes. Scrape down the sides of the bowl with a rubber spatula and beat for another 2 minutes. Using a large spoon stir in the remaining 1¼ cups flour. The dough will be medium soft, slightly softer than bread dough.

Turn the dough out on to a lightly floured surface and knead for 5 minutes or until the dough is smooth and elastic. Shape into a ball and place in a lightly oiled bowl, turn to coat the dough with oil and cover with plastic wrap. Refrigerate a minimum of 5 hours and up to 2 days.

To make the filling: Combine all the filling ingredients in a small bowl and rub together with fingers until well mixed.

To assemble the rolls: Place the dough on a lightly floured surface and knead about 2 minutes. Cover the dough and let it rest for 30 minutes.

Using a rolling pin, roll the dough into a 14 x 10 rectangle. Add more flour if the dough is sticky. After the dough is rolled out, sprinkle with filling, leaving a ¼-inch border at the edges. Start rolling the dough into a log shape at the long side of the rectangle. Pinch the seams to seal. Cut into 12 equal pieces. Place the rolls, cut-side up, in a well-oiled 9-inch round cake pan. Cover with a clean dish towel and allow to rise in a draft-free location for 45 minutes or until doubled in size.

Preheat oven to 350°F. Bake the rolls for 22–27 minutes or until golden brown. Allow to cool 10 minutes on a wire rack.

Run a metal spatula around the edge of the pan and invert onto a plate. Using another plate, invert again so the rolls are right-side up.

To make the glaze: Combine all glaze ingredients in a small bowl and whisk until smooth. Drizzle the glaze over the tops of the buns and serve.

Cover any unused rolls. To reheat, wrap loosely in foil and bake at 200°F for 10–15 minutes.

Makes 12 cinnamon rolls.

Blueberry Almond Coffeecake

Nothing beats this blueberry delight on a sunny Sunday morning!

Topping:
½   cup oats
¼   cup all-purpose flour
¼   cup brown sugar, packed
⅓   cup slivered almonds
½   teaspoon cinnamon
2   tablespoons olive oil

1¼   cups all-purpose flour
1   cup whole wheat pastry flour

½   teaspoon salt
2   teaspoons baking powder
1   egg
¾   cup granulated sugar
⅓   cup olive oil
1   teaspoon vanilla extract
1½   teaspoons almond extract
½   cup low-fat or fat-free milk
1½   cups blueberries, fresh or frozen

If using frozen berries, allow them to thaw slightly, about 15 minutes on a large plate.

Preheat oven to 350°F and lightly oil an 8 x 8-inch glass baking dish.

To make the topping: Mix oats, flour, brown sugar, and cinnamon in a small bowl. Add the olive oil and using fingers, rub together until the mixture starts to come together. Add almonds and combine. Set aside.

To make the cake: In a small bowl mix both kinds of flour, salt, and baking powder and set aside. In a large bowl, beat the egg and sugar with a handheld mixer until light in color and thickened, then add the olive oil and beat for 2 minutes. Add the vanilla and almond extracts and milk; beat to incorporate. Using a large spoon stir in the dry ingredients until nearly smooth, then add the blueberries and continue to stir until batter is well-mixed.

Transfer batter to prepared baking dish and spread evenly. Sprinkle evenly with topping mixture.

Bake for 35–40 minutes or until toothpick inserted into the center comes out clean.

Cool in pan on a wire rack. Cut into 9 pieces. Can be served warm or room temperature.

Makes 9 servings.

Cinnamon Coffeecake

Cinnamon, one of the earliest known spices, is the dried inner bark of a genus of evergreen tree common in south and east Asia. The Romans believed cinnamon was sacred. Because cinnamon was so heavily sought in the fifteenth century by European explorers, some say it indirectly led to the discovery of America. This incredible coffeecake honors the distinguished spice's long history.

1½ cups all-purpose flour	¾ cup olive oil
1 cup whole wheat pastry flour	1½ teaspoons baking powder
¾ cup brown sugar, packed	1 teaspoon baking soda
¾ cup granulated sugar	1 cup low-fat buttermilk
2½ teaspoons plus ¾ teaspoon cinnamon	1 egg, beaten
1½ teaspoons ginger	¾ cup chopped walnuts
½ teaspoon salt	

Preheat oven to 350°F and spray a 9 x 13-inch baking dish with cooking spray.

In a large bowl, combine flours, brown and granulated sugars, 2½ teaspoons cinnamon, ginger, and salt. Then add the olive oil, and using fingers, rub together until the mixture has a crumb-like texture. Reserve ½ cup of this mixture in a small bowl. Add baking powder and baking soda to the remaining mixture and blend. Then add the buttermilk and egg and stir to combine.

To the small bowl with the reserved ½ cup of crumb mixture, add walnuts and ¾ teaspoon cinnamon. Set this mixture aside.

Transfer the batter to the prepared pan and sprinkle with the nut mixture.

Bake for 32–36 minutes or until a toothpick inserted into the center comes out clean.

Cool in the pan on a wire rack.

Serves 10–12.

Maple Apple Pecan Coffeecake

Pecans, like many other nuts, are high in healthy monounsaturated fats and vitamins. Add pecans, walnuts, and almonds to your snack food shelf. Mixed nuts are best eaten fresh, of course, so look to buy in small quantities from the refrigerated section at a food co-op.

1½	cups peeled, thinly sliced apples (Granny Smith is a good choice; about 1 large apple).	2	tablespoons olive oil
3	tablespoons brown sugar	1	large egg
1	tablespoon real maple syrup	½	teaspoon vanilla extract
⅛	teaspoon maple extract	1	teaspoon maple extract
½	teaspoon ground cinnamon	½	cup low-fat or fat-free buttermilk
1	cup all-purpose flour	2	tablespoons chopped pecans
½	teaspoon baking soda		*Glaze: (optional)*
⅛	teaspoon salt	¼	cup sifted powdered sugar
⅓	cup granulated sugar	1	teaspoon low-fat or fat-free buttermilk
		¼	teaspoon vanilla extract

Preheat oven to 350°F. Spray an 8-inch square cake pan with cooking spray.

To prepare the cake: Combine the apple slices, brown sugar, maple syrup, maple extract, and cinnamon in a small saucepan over medium-high heat. Cook 5 minutes or until syrupy, stirring frequently; cool.

In a small bowl, combine flour, baking soda, and salt, stirring well with a whisk. In another large bowl, combine granulated sugar and olive oil; beat with a mixer at medium speed until well blended. Add egg and vanilla and maple extracts, beating well. Add flour mixture to sugar mixture alternately with buttermilk, beginning and ending with flour mixture; beat well after each addition.

Spoon the batter into an prepared cake pan. Arrange apple mixture over cake, lightly drizzling any remaining syrup over batter.

Bake for 25 minutes or until cake begins to pull away from sides of pan. Cool in pan on a wire rack for 10 minutes.

To make the glaze: In a small bowl, combine powdered sugar, 1 teaspoon buttermilk, and ¼ teaspoon vanilla; stir with a whisk. Drizzle glaze over cake. Sprinkle with pecans.

Serve warm or at room temperature.

Makes 8 servings.

Mocha Coffeecake

This great, quick cake does double duty as both a coffeecake and a dessert. It is rich and flavorful without being too sweet.

Topping:

⅓ cup brown sugar, packed
¼ cup semisweet mini chocolate chips
1 tablespoon unsweetened cocoa powder, sifted

¾ cup all-purpose flour
½ cup whole wheat pastry flour
1¼ cups granulated sugar
¼ teaspoon salt

1½ teaspoons baking powder
½ teaspoon baking soda
⅓ cup unsweetened cocoa powder, sifted
3 eggs
⅔ cup low-fat or fat-free sour cream
¼ cup olive oil
⅓ cup brewed coffee, cold or room temperature
1 tablespoon instant coffee granules
1 teaspoon vanilla extract

To make the topping: In a small bowl, combine all of the topping ingredients: brown sugar, chocolate chips, and cocoa. Set aside.

Preheat oven to 350°F and coat a 9-inch square glass baking dish with cooking spray.

In a large bowl, combine flours, sugar, salt, baking powder, baking soda, and cocoa powder. Make a well in the center.

In a separate bowl, whisk together eggs, sour cream, olive oil, coffee, instant coffee, and vanilla extract. Pour the wet ingredients into the well in the center of the dry. Stir just until the mixture is combined.

Pour the batter into the prepared pan. Sprinkle with the topping.

Bake for 30–40 minutes or until a toothpick inserted into the center comes out clean.

Cool on a wire rack. Serve warm or at room temperature.

Serves 9–12.

Pear Coffeecake with Ginger and Pecans

Pears are rich in dietary fiber, vitamins, and minerals. They are excellent for eating out of hand and in salads. This moist coffeecake showcases pears and pecans with nutmeg and ginger. Bartletts are my favorite choice for this recipe, as they are succulent and sweet.

1½	cups all-purpose flour	1	egg, beaten
1	cup whole wheat pastry flour	2	teaspoons vanilla extract
¾	cup granulated sugar	1	cup low-fat or fat-free buttermilk, shaken
1	cup dark brown sugar	1½	cups peeled, diced pears (2–3 pears)
1	teaspoon salt		*Topping:*
½	teaspoon freshly ground nutmeg	½	teaspoon ground ginger or 1 tablespoon minced crystallized ginger
⅔	cup olive oil	1	cup chopped pecans
1	teaspoon baking soda		
1	teaspoon baking powder		

Preheat oven to 350°F and coat a 9 x 13-inch sheet pan with cooking spray.

Mix together the flours, sugars, salt, nutmeg, and olive oil. Reserve 1 cup of this mixture for the topping. Add the baking soda and baking powder to the remaining crumb mixture. Then stir in the egg, vanilla, buttermilk, and the pears.

To the reserved 1 cup crumb mixture, add the ginger and pecans.

Transfer the batter to the prepared baking pan and sprinkle with topping.

Bake for 40–45 minutes or until a toothpick inserted into the center of the cake comes out clean.

Cool in the pan on a wire rack.

Serve warm or at room temperature.

Makes 14–18 servings.

Wide-Awake Espresso Coffeecake

Calling all coffee lovers—this cake is for you! It is easy enough to whip up in a pinch for unexpected company.

¼	cup brown sugar, packed	2	large eggs
1	teaspoon ground cinnamon	⅔	cup fat-free vanilla yogurt
½	cup semisweet mini chocolate chips	2	teaspoons vanilla extract
1	tablespoon instant espresso or 2 tablespoons instant coffee granules, divided	1⅓	cups all-purpose flour
⅓	cup olive oil	½	teaspoon baking soda
1	cup granulated sugar	¼	teaspoon salt

Preheat oven to 350°F. Coat an 8-inch square baking pan with cooking spray.

In a small bowl combine brown sugar, cinnamon, chocolate chips, and 1 teaspoon espresso granules.

In a large bowl, combine olive oil and granulated sugar, stirring with a whisk. Add eggs; stir well. Stir in yogurt and vanilla. Set aside.

Lightly spoon 1⅓ cups flour into dry measuring cups and level with a knife. Combine flour, baking soda, salt, and remaining 2 teaspoons espresso powder in a small bowl. Add dry ingredients to the wet, stirring just until blended.

Spread half of the batter into the prepared pan and sprinkle with half of the brown sugar mixture. Carefully spread remaining batter over brown sugar mixture and sprinkle with remaining brown sugar mixture.

Bake for 25 minutes or until a toothpick inserted in center comes out clean.

Cool for 10 minutes in pan on a wire rack. Cut into squares.

Serve warm or at room temperature. Store any leftovers in a covered container.

Serves 9.

CHAPTER 10
SAVORY BREADS

Classic Pizza Dough

There is nothing more fun and satisfying than making your own pizza. Start with this basic dough and go wild with all kinds of creative and innovative toppings. Let the kids help and make "Family Pizza Night" a tradition in your home.

2	cups warm water (between 105° and 115°F)	¼	cup olive oil
		2	teaspoons salt
4½	teaspoons yeast or 2 packets of dry active yeast	⅛–¼	teaspoon freshly ground black pepper
		1½	cups whole wheat pastry or bread flour
I	teaspoon granulated sugar	3–3½	cups all-purpose flour

Combine the water, yeast, and sugar in a large bowl and whisk to dissolve the yeast. Allow the yeast to rest for 10 minutes or until foamy.

Using a large whisk or a wooden spoon stir in olive oil, salt, pepper, and whole wheat flour. Whisk until batter is well combined. Add 2 cups all-purpose flour and stir until dough resembles a thick batter. Add additional flour ½ cup at a time until you have a dough that is slightly sticky.

Turn the dough out onto a well-floured surface and knead until it is smooth and elastic, about 10 minutes. Add more flour as necessary to prevent the dough from sticking to your hands or the surface.

After the dough has reached the desired texture, place in a well-oiled bowl, turning the dough to coat. Cover the dough with a clean kitchen towel and let rise in a draft-free location until doubled in bulk, about 45 minutes.

After the dough has risen, turn it out onto a floured surface and divide in two. Knead lightly and form dough into two balls. Let rest 5 minutes. Working with one ball of dough at a time, flatten the dough, working from the center to the edge. If holes develop, pinch that area back together. You can make a thick or thin crust pizza, between ¼- and ½-inch thick. Keep in mind that the crust will rise in the oven.

This recipe will make 2 medium pizza crusts.

Add toppings and bake at 400°F until light brown and bubbly. Or prebake the crust at 400°F for 8–10 minutes or until it is light brown on the bottom. This is a good idea if you are using a lot of wet ingredients or prefer a crisper crust.

Makes 2 crusts.

Dilly Irish Soda Bread

This bread is easy to make and is the perfect companion for a bowl of hearty bean soup on a cold winter day. Traditionally, Irish soda bread used sour milk, but today buttermilk is used since it is easily found. (You can also use buttermilk in things like pancakes.) You can make your own sour milk by combining two cups of fresh milk with 1 tablespoon of lemon juice or distilled vinegar. In about 15 minutes you will notice a distinctive change in the texture of the milk. Use this as a substitute for buttermilk.

3 cups whole wheat pastry flour	1 tablespoon dill seeds, bruised with a mortar and pestle
1¾ teaspoons salt	
1 tablespoon sugar	1½ cups low-fat buttermilk, shaken, or sour milk
1 teaspoon baking soda	
½ teaspoon baking powder	3 tablespoons olive oil

Preheat oven to 375°F and coat an 8- or 9-inch glass pie plate with cooking spray.

In a large bowl, combine flour, salt, sugar, baking soda, baking powder, and dill seeds. Make a well in the center of the dry ingredients.

In a separate bowl, combine the buttermilk and olive oil. Add this mixture to the dry ingredients and stir just until combined.

Transfer the dough to the prepared baking dish and form into a loaf shape with hands coated with additional olive oil.

Bake bread for 55–65 minutes or until it is golden and sounds hollow when tapped on the bottom.

Transfer the bread to a rack and allow to cool.

Makes 1 loaf.

Fougasse with Herbes de Provence

This recipe for fougasse, the French version of the Italian focaccia bread, is topped with mixed herbes de Provence. The flat bread can be slashed to form shapes such as a leaf, tree, or wheat stalk, or the slits can be cut to form a lattice, making the bread easy to pull apart. The results can be truly impressive!

1½	cups warm water (about 110°)	1	tablespoon herbes de Provence*
1	teaspoon dry yeast	2	teaspoons sea salt, plus additional for sprinkling on top
½	teaspoon granulated sugar		
2	cups all-purpose flour	4	tablespoons olive oil, divided use
2	cups whole wheat pastry flour	¼	cup yellow cornmeal

Pour water into a large bowl. Sprinkle yeast and sugar into water and stir until dissolved and yeast is activated, about 8–10 minutes.

Combine the two flours in a small bowl. In a large bowl, place 1 cup of the combined flours, 1 tablespoon herbes, sea salt, and 2 tablespoons olive oil and stir until well blended. Continue to stir in the flour, 1 cup at a time, until a thick and somewhat sticky dough forms.

Turn the dough out onto a lightly floured surface and knead until smooth and elastic, about 6–8 minutes. Form the dough into a ball and place into an oiled bowl. Turn the dough to coat the surface. Cover the bowl with a clean dishtowel and let it rise in a draft-free location until doubled, about 1 hour.

Punch dough down and divide in half. Shape into irregular ovals, about 1½ inch thick. Sprinkle cornmeal over 2 baking sheets; transfer dough to pans. Brush each loaf with olive oil, and sprinkle the remaining herbs on top. Make several slashes in the bread, cutting through the dough with a knife. Cover the loaves with clean dishtowels. Let rise again, about 20 minutes.

Place baking sheets into a preheated 450°F oven. Quickly splash a small amount of water onto the floor of your oven to create steam and close the oven door. Bake until golden, about 20 minutes.

*Note: If you don't have dried herbes de Provence, substitute this herb mixture:

½ tablespoon dried basil
½ tablespoon ground savory
½ tablespoon dried thyme
½ tablespoon dried rosemary

DAIRY-FREE

Makes 2 loaves.

Garlic-Onion Crescent Rolls

1	cup warm water (110°F), divided	2	cups whole wheat pastry flour
1	envelope dry yeast or 2¼ teaspoons dry yeast	4	tablespoons olive oil
1½	teaspoons granulated sugar	2½	teaspoons sea salt
1	cup lukewarm milk	2	tablespoons olive oil
1	egg	3	cups finely chopped onions
3	cups all-purpose flour	5	large cloves garlic, minced

Pour ¼ cup of warm water into large bowl and sprinkle yeast and sugar over. Stir to blend and let stand until yeast dissolves and begins to bubble, about 10 minutes. Add ¾ cup warm water, lukewarm milk, and 1 egg to the yeast mixture and whisk to blend.

Combine both flours in a medium bowl and mix. Add 3 cups of the flour mixture to the yeast mixture and stir vigorously with wooden spoon until smooth thick batter forms, about 2 minutes. Cover bowl with kitchen towel and let batter rest for 15 minutes.

Stir 4 tablespoons olive oil and salt into batter. Add remaining flour mixture to batter ½ cup at a time, mixing using a wooden spoon, until smooth dough forms. Turn dough out onto floured work surface, and knead until dough is smooth and elastic, about 10 minutes. Add flour if dough is too sticky.

Form dough into ball and place in a large, oiled bowl. Turn dough to coat with olive oil and cover with a clean dish towel. Let dough rise in warm, draft-free area until doubled in volume, about 1 hour 15 minutes.

Meanwhile, sauté the onions in 2 tablespoons olive oil until very tender, about 15 minutes. Add minced garlic and sauté another 5 minutes. Set aside to cool completely.

Punch down dough and turn out onto floured work surface. Divide dough in half and knead each half into ball. Cover loosely with towel and let rest on floured surface 10 minutes.

Using rolling pin, roll 1 dough ball to 14-inch round. Spread half of onions on top, leaving 1-inch outside border. Cut dough round into 8 wedges, using a pizza cutter. Starting at wide end of each wedge, roll up toward point. Place rolls on greased, heavy, large baking sheet, shaping into crescents and spacing evenly. Loosely cover rolls with towel. Repeat with remaining dough ball and onions. Let rolls rise in warm, draft-free area until almost doubled in volume, about 30 minutes.

Preheat oven to 375°F. Bake both sheets at once, switching position after 12 minutes. Continue baking for another 12 minutes. Total baking time is about 24–28 minutes or until golden brown.

Transfer rolls to racks and cool. Can be made 2 weeks ahead. Wrap in foil; freeze.

Makes 16 rolls.

Oatmeal Honey Bread

Pair this bread with a hearty soup. It is a great alternative to cornbread.

I	cup whole wheat pastry flour	¼	cup honey
I	cup quick-cooking oats	I	cup low-fat milk
I	tablespoon baking powder	I	egg
½	teaspoon salt	¼	cup olive oil

Preheat oven to 400°F. Coat a 9-inch round or square baking pan with cooking spray.

In a large bowl, combine the flour, oats, baking powder, and salt. Make a well in the center.

In a separate bowl, combine the honey, milk, egg, and olive oil.

Pour the wet ingredients into the well in the dry and stir just until moistened. Do not over-mix.

Transfer batter to the prepared pan.

Bake for 15–20 minutes. Cool in pan for 5 minutes, then transfer to a wire rack. Let cool or serve warm.

Makes 6–8 servings.

Spicy Cheese Flat Bread Wedges

These are great for any event . . . and they are fun to make!

Dough:

1 cup warm water (about 105°–115°F)
2 teaspoons granulated sugar
2¼ teaspoons active dry yeast (or one packet)
3 tablespoons olive oil
1½ teaspoons salt
1 cup whole wheat pastry flour
1¾–2 cups all-purpose flour

Topping:

1 teaspoon dried basil
2 teaspoons dried oregano
2 fresh, finely minced garlic cloves
½ teaspoon freshly ground black pepper
½ teaspoon kosher salt
4 tablespoons olive oil

2 cups shredded mozzarella cheese, divided

Put the warm water in a large bowl; sprinkle sugar and yeast over the water. Whisk to dissolve the yeast and let sit for about 10 minutes. Once the yeast has begun to grow, add the olive oil and salt.

Stir in the whole wheat pastry flour and ½ cup of the all-purpose flour. After this has been well-combined, add more flour, ¼ cup at a time, to the dough. Once a total of 2½ cups of flour have been incorporated into the dough, turn it out on to a bread board or a clean surface sprinkled lightly with flour.

The dough will be sticky. Sprinkle with additional flour and knead until smooth and elastic, about 10 minutes. After the kneading is over, divide the dough into 8 pieces and roll them into balls. Place the balls on a well-oiled baking sheet and roll them in the oil to coat. Cover with a clean towel and allow to rest in a draft-free location for 30 minutes.

To make the topping: Place the basil, oregano, garlic, pepper, salt, and olive oil in a small bowl and stir.

To make the flat bread: Take one of the dough balls and flatten with fingers into a circle, about 6–8 inches. Or you can place the dough between two sheets of plastic wrap and roll out with a rolling pin.

Preheat oven to 400°F.

After the dough is in a circular shape, about ¼ inch thick, place on a large, oiled baking sheet. Using the back of a spoon, coat the dough evenly with a thin layer of the topping.

Sprinkle with ¼ cup mozzarella cheese and bake for 15 minutes.

Cut into wedges and serve warm.

Makes 8 flat breads, enough appetizers for 8–10 people.

Zucchini Corn Fritters

These yummy fritters are a family favorite and a great way to showcase summer's bounty. Serve them warm with guacamole or sour cream.

2	cups all-purpose flour		¼	cup olive oil
1	tablespoon baking powder		2	cups finely shredded zucchini
½	teaspoon ground cumin		1½	cups fresh corn kernels, cut from the cob
⅛	teaspoon ground red pepper, or to taste		1	tablespoon finely chopped cilantro
¼	cup granulated sugar		1	cup finely grated sharp cheddar cheese
1	teaspoon salt			Sour cream or guacamole
¼	teaspoon freshly ground black pepper			Scallions, thinly sliced
2	eggs, lightly beaten			Oil for frying or cooking spray
1	cup milk			

In a large bowl, stir together flour, baking powder, cumin, red pepper, sugar, salt, and black pepper.

In a small bowl, whisk together eggs, milk, and olive oil. Whisk the wet ingredients into the dry, just until combined. Stir in the zucchini, corn, cilantro, and cheddar cheese.

Preheat a cast iron skillet or griddle to medium-high. Oil lightly. Drop batter by the tablespoonful onto the griddle. Fry until crisp and brown, turning once.

Remove to paper towels.

Serve warm with sour cream or guacamole and thinly sliced scallions.

Makes 5 dozen appetizer-size fritters.

CHAPTER 11
OTHER TASTY TREATS

Chocolate Peppermint Bark

This is the ideal gift or treat for the holiday season. The balance of chocolate and mint is divine!

1	cup all-purpose flour		1	teaspoon instant coffee
½	cup whole wheat pastry flour		2	teaspoons vanilla
¾	teaspoon baking soda		3	tablespoons water
½	teaspoon salt		½	cup plus 1 tablespoon olive oil
½	cup unsweetened cocoa powder, sifted		1¼	cups chocolate chips
½	cup brown sugar, packed		¾	cup crushed candy canes or peppermint
¾	cup granulated sugar			hard candies

Preheat oven to 350°F. Line two baking sheets with parchment paper.

In a large bowl, combine the flours, baking soda, salt, and cocoa powder.

In another bowl, whisk together the sugars, instant coffee, vanilla, water, and olive oil. Stir the wet ingredients into the dry until a thick dough forms.

Divide the dough in half, and using either an off-set spatula or your hands, press the dough to a thickness of slightly less than ¼ inch. The dough does not have to fit to the edges of the pan, but be sure that it is evenly thin.

Bake for 18–20 minutes or until the dough is slightly firm and has a dull look to the surface.

After it has been removed from the oven, sprinkle the chocolate chips on the top. Allow to sit for 5 minutes or until the chips look melted. Spread the melted chocolate over the surface of the cookie with a spatula or the back of a large spoon. Immediately sprinkle with crushed candy.

Set in a cool location to allow the chocolate to harden. Once the chocolate is completely hardened, break into small pieces, about 2 x 2 inches.

Store in an airtight container.

Makes 36–40 pieces.

DAILY TREE

Nutty Fruit Granola

Homemade granola can't be beat—almost anything goes, so get creative.

6	cups old-fashioned rolled oats (approx. 18 oz.)	¼	cup light brown sugar, packed
1	cup unsalted, shelled sunflower seeds	1	teaspoon cinnamon
¼	sesame seeds	1	cup raisins
½	cup slivered almonds	¾	cup chopped dried apples
⅔	cup olive oil	½	cup each dried cranberries, cherries, and blueberries
⅔	cup honey		

Preheat oven to 350°F. Set out two large baking pans.

In a large bowl, combine oats, sunflower seeds, sesame seeds, and almonds. Set aside.

In a medium bowl, whisk together olive oil, honey, brown sugar, and cinnamon. It will not want to combine well and will have a tendency to separate. Poor the honey-oil mixture over the oat mixture and toss with your hands, mixing well. Be sure to coat all of the dry mixture.

Divide the granola between the two pans.

Bake for 25–30 minutes total or until golden and lightly toasted. Stir the granola and switch position of the pans in the oven every 10 minutes.

Cool on the pans for 10 minutes and then transfer to a tray lined with waxed paper.

After completely cool, stir in fruit and store in an airtight container for up 2 months.

Makes 5 cups.

DAIRY-FREE

Super Seed Granola

Maple syrup adds a wonderful sweetness to this wholesome snack. If you want to add some dried fruit to the mixture, do so after it is baked and completely cool. Then store the granola in the freezer to prevent the moisture from the fruit making the grains wet. Great with yogurt or stirred into pancakes.

3	cups old-fashioned rolled oats	½	teaspoon cinnamon
1	cup sweetened flaked coconut	¼	teaspoon salt
½	cup hulled pumpkin seeds (pepitas)	½	cup olive oil
¼	cup flax seeds	½	cup pure maple syrup
¼	cup sesame seeds	½	cup brown sugar, packed
½	cup chopped walnuts		Dried fruit (optional)
½	cup unsalted sunflower seeds		

Preheat oven to 350°F.

In a large bowl, combine oats, coconut, pumpkin seeds, flax seeds, sesame seeds, walnuts, sunflower seeds, cinnamon, and salt. Set aside.

In a medium bowl, whisk together olive oil, maple syrup, and brown sugar. It will not want to combine well and will have a tendency to separate. Pour the maple-oil mixture over the oat mixture, and with your hands, toss and mix well. Be sure to coat all of the dry mixture.

Spread the granola in an even layer in an approximately 10 x 15-inch sheet pan.

Bake at 350°F for 30–40 minutes or until golden and lightly toasted. Stir the granola occasionally.

Cool on the pans for 5 minutes and then transfer to a tray lined with parchment or waxed paper.

After completely cool, stir in dried fruit, if desired. Store in an airtight container for up 2 months.

Makes 6 cups.

DAIRY-FREE/VEGAN

Toffee Crunch Brittle

While some might argue that this treat is a cookie, it seems more like candy to me. The flavor is rich without being heavy. As a gift anytime or at the holidays, you can't go wrong. Make sure it is completely cool before you pack it away.

1	cup all-purpose flour	2	teaspoons vanilla extract
½	cup whole wheat pastry flour	2	tablespoons water
½	teaspoon baking soda	⅔	cup olive oil
½	teaspoon salt	1½	cups chocolate-covered toffee bits or
½	cup granulated sugar		crushed candy bars
⅓	cup brown sugar, packed	1	cup chopped walnuts

Preheat oven to 350°F and line a 10 x 15-inch baking sheet with parchment paper.

In a small bowl, combine the flours, baking soda, and salt.

In a large bowl, whisk together the sugars, vanilla extract, water, and olive oil. Add the dry ingredients to the wet and stir to combine.

Add the toffee bits and the nuts and mix. The dough will be crumb-like. Press the dough into the prepared pan.

Bake for 20–22 minutes or until the edges are slightly brown and the cookie is firm to the touch.

Cool 10 minutes in the pan. Lifting by the edge of the parchment, remove to a wire rack to cool completely.

Break the cooled cookie into 4- or 5-inch chunks. Store in an airtight container at room temperature up to 5 days.

Makes 24+ servings.

DAIRY-FREE VEGAN

Appendix

Recipe Conversion

Perhaps you have some favorite family recipes that could be updated and made a little (or a lot) healthier. Let's take a look at some ways that you can adapt a recipe to include whole grains, olive oil, or more fruit and nuts.

I love going to the kitchen with just an idea and then putting it into action. The more I experiment, the more confident I become at controlling the chemistry of baking and understanding the interaction of raw ingredients. There are so many factors that can affect baking—weather, the temperature of your ingredients, and the mechanics of preparation such as stirring and sifting. That is what makes baking fun and sometimes surprising. It is performance art in many ways.

If an experimental style of baking is foreign to you, start slowly and keep in mind the following:

- Resist the temptation to completely overhaul a recipe on the first try. Instead, make one or two changes at a time, and see if you like the effect.
- Experiment when you are not under pressure. The time for experimentation is not the night you are hosting a dinner party or making cookies for a bake sale. Some bakers work well under stress and uncertainty and can usually rise to the occasion, but for most of us this performance pressure is just painful.
- Most experiments do not come out exactly as expected, so try not to have too many expectations, and be ready to accept the occasional unexpected outcome.
- Even the most talented baker will experience failures—try to learn from them. And then again, sometimes things will turn out better than expected.
- Relax and enjoy the process!

Some ideas to keep in mind when converting recipes to use olive oil:

- Be sure to use less olive oil in the recipe than the amount of butter you are replacing.
- If a recipe calls for more than ½ cup butter, start by trying a combination of one-half butter and one-half olive oil in order to help maintain the original texture of the item.
- Generally speaking, cookies made with olive oil take slightly longer to bake than cookies made with butter or margarine. Keep an eye on your cookies. Better to be vigilant than remorseful.

- Cookies baked with olive oil also tend to be slightly lighter in color than butter cookies—again, be careful not to overbake.
- The texture of raw dough made with olive oil tends to be a bit softer than butter doughs.
- It is easy to balance the flavor of virgin olive oil in delicately flavored baked goods by adjusting spices and flavorings, such as vanilla and almond extract.

Nestlé® Toll House® Chocolate Chip Cookies

One recipe that people ask me to adapt for them is the classic Toll House® Chocolate Chip Cookie. Here is the recipe as written on the package:

2¼ cups all-purpose flour
1   teaspoon baking soda
1   teaspoon salt
1   cup (2 sticks or ½ pound) butter, softened
¾   cup granulated [white] sugar
¾   cup packed brown sugar
1   teaspoon vanilla extract
2   eggs
2   cups (one 12-ounce package) Nestlé® Toll House® Semi-Sweet Chocolate Morsels
1   cup chopped nuts

Combine flour, baking soda, and salt in small bowl. Beat butter, granulated sugar, brown sugar, and vanilla in large mixing bowl. Add eggs, one at a time, beating well after each addition; gradually beat in flour mixture. Stir in morsels and nuts. Drop by rounded tablespoon onto ungreased baking sheets.

Bake in preheated 375°F oven for 9–11 minutes or until golden brown. Let stand for 2 minutes; remove to wire racks to cool completely.

Makes 2½ dozen cookies.

And here are some healthy changes we can make:
- Include some whole wheat pastry flour and a bit of wheat germ. I like to use a combination of all-purpose flour and whole wheat pastry flour because I've found that this helps to retain more of the original appearance and texture of the cookie. Wheat germ is not noticeable in the final product and adds some flavor and fiber.

- Adding a bit more pure vanilla extract makes all the difference in the world with this cookie—so add ½ teaspoon more, for a total of 1½ teaspoons.
- Change the 2 sticks of butter to 1 stick and ⅓ cup of olive oil.
- If you prefer a slightly cakier cookie, change the sugar ratio of granulated to brown slightly. Generally, I like the less-chewy texture produced when there is 1 cup of granulated sugar and ½ cup of light brown sugar.
- Two cups of chocolate chips are more than enough—in my eyes it is too much, actually. When I make this recipe, generally I use 1 cup or slightly more. I leave the 1 cup of nuts unchanged.

And here is my modified recipe:

Lisa's Chocolate Chip Cookies

1½	cups all-purpose flour	½	cup brown sugar, packed
1	cup whole wheat pastry flour	⅓	cup olive oil
2	tablespoons wheat germ	2	teaspoons vanilla
1	teaspoon baking soda	2	eggs
1	teaspoon salt	1–1½	cups chocolate chips
1	stick butter, softened	1	cup chopped walnuts
1	cup granulated sugar		

Preheat oven to 375°F. In a small bowl, combine the flours, wheat germ, baking soda, and salt and set aside.

In another bowl using a handheld mixer, beat together the softened butter, granulated sugar, and brown sugar. Add the olive oil, vanilla, and eggs and beat until light and fluffy.

Stir the dry ingredients into the wet until combined. Then stir in the chocolate chips and walnuts.

Drop by rounded spoonful onto cookie sheets. Bake for 12–14 minutes or until slightly brown at the edges. Do not overbake. Allow to cool on the sheet for 2 minutes and then transfer to a wire rack to cool completely.

Makes about 3 dozen cookies.

Betty Crocker Snickerdoodles:

Growing up, the Betty Crocker cookbook was the gold standard for all things baking. The page with the snickerdoodle recipe was dusted with flour and had developed a rather leathery texture from many years of use. The distinctive taste of this cookie has stayed with me as a reminder of childhood and the rattle of the cookie jar.

I	cup soft shortening
I½	cups sugar
2	eggs
2¾	cups all purpose flour, sifted
2	teaspoons cream of tartar
I	teaspoon soda
½	teaspoon salt
2	tablespoons sugar
2	teaspoons cinnamon

Mix together the shortening, sugar and eggs thoroughly. Stir in the flour, cream of tartar, soda and salt. Chill the dough. Roll into balls the size of small walnuts. Roll in a mixture of 2 tablespoons sugar and 2 teaspoons cinnamon. Place about 2″ apart on an ungreased baking sheet. Bake at 400° for 8–10 minutes or until lightly browned. Makes about 5 dozen cookies.

And here is my modified recipe:

Lisa's Snickerdoodles

2	cups all-purpose flour	⅓	cup olive oil
I	cup whole wheat pastry flour	I⅓	cups sugar
2	teaspoons cream of tartar	2	eggs
I	teaspoon baking soda	½	teaspoon vanilla extract
½	teaspoon salt	2	tablespoons sugar
½	cup butter, softened	2	teaspoons cinnamon

Preheat oven to 375°F degrees. In a small bowl, combine the flours, cream of tartar, baking soda, and salt.

In a large bowl, combine the butter, olive oil, sugar, eggs, and vanilla extract. Stir using a large spoon until thoroughly mixed. Add the dry ingredients.

Chill the dough. Roll into balls the size of small walnuts. Roll in a mixture of 2 tablespoons sugar and 2 teaspoons cinnamon. Place about 2″ apart on an ungreased baking sheet. Bake for 10–12 minutes or until lightly browned.

Makes about 5 dozen cookies.

Taster's Choice Coffee Cookies

This recipe was the inspiration for my Chocolate Coffee Cookies.

1½	cups all purpose flour	¼	cup granulated sugar
4	teaspoons unsweetened baking cocoa	I	egg
½	teaspoon baking soda	I	teaspoon vanilla extract
¼	teaspoon salt	5	tablespoons instant coffee crystals
½	cup butter, softened	2	tablespoons hot water
½	cup brown sugar, packed	I	cup chocolate chips

Preheat oven to 350°F. Lightly grease baking sheets.

In a small bowl combine flour, cocoa, baking soda, and salt. Beat butter, brown sugar, and granulated sugar in large mixer bowl until light and creamy. Beat in egg and vanilla extract.

Combine instant coffee and water in small bowl; stir until coffee is dissolved. Add to sugar mixture; mix well. Gradually mix in flour mixture. Stir in chocolate chips. Drop by rounded teaspoon onto prepared baking sheets.

Bake for 10–12 minutes or until edges are crisp. Remove to wire racks to cool completely.

And here is my modified recipe (I have doubled the recipe in this conversion; it seems to work out better):

Lisa's Chocolate Coffee Cookies

These cookies have been sent across the country in care packages, taken to family members at the birth of a child, and enjoyed by people of all ages. The smell is truly divine. And despite my best efforts, this is one recipe that I have not been able to convert entirely to olive oil with the same results. I have, however, been able to make this recipe much healthier and, in my eyes, a bit tastier.

1½	cups all-purpose flour	1	cup brown sugar, packed
1½	cups whole wheat pastry flour	½	cup granulated sugar
¼	cup unsweetened baking cocoa	2	eggs
1	teaspoon baking soda	2½	teaspoons vanilla
½	teaspoon salt	8	tablespoons instant coffee
½	cup butter, softened	3	tablespoons hot water
⅓	cup olive oil	1½	cups semisweet chocolate chips

Preheat oven to 350°F.

Combine flours, cocoa, baking soda, and salt in a small bowl. Beat butter, olive oil, brown sugar, and granulated sugar in large mixer bowl until light and creamy. Beat in eggs and vanilla extract.

Combine instant coffee and water in small bowl; stir until coffee is dissolved. Add to sugar mixture; mix well. Gradually mix in flour mixture. Stir in chocolate chips. Drop by rounded teaspoonfuls onto prepared baking sheets.

Bake for 12–13 minutes or until the centers are puffed and the cookies look slightly underdone.

Cool on the pan for 3–4 minutes and then remove to wire racks to cool completely. If you like cookies that are crisp, rather than soft and chewy, bake for about 2 minutes longer.

Makes 4–5 dozen cookies.

Index

W

Z